A CHILD OF

LOVE AND WAR

Also by D.M.Thomas:

See also dmthomasonline.net

A CHILD OF

LOVE AND WAR

verse memoir

D.M. THOMAS

The Cornovia Press

SHEFFIELD

Published by The Cornovia Press, Sheffield, 2021

ISBN 978-1-908878-23-6

Contents

Author's Note

This is not a record of facts but of important relationships in the emotional and sexual sphere. They are viewed from my perspective, and therefore unreliably. The period covered is from 1935 to 1998, when I was 63.

DMT, Truro, 2021

'Another life, a distant shore...'
  – Pushkin, lyric.

'There are four of us'
  – Akhmatova, lyric

One

Four of us

1

Women... It's all I've ever thought of,

Except for the odd hour or two;

In age, you'd think I might have fought off

Obsession with them, burnt it through,

But no, it stays; so too, a feature

Observed by the close friend of Nietzsche

And brilliant female analyst

Lou Andreas-Salomé: 'Men can invest

With unimaginable splendour

A woman's hair, shoes, corset, gloves',

Early life choosing what we love.

It's rarer in the female gender.

For me, my fledgling psyche chose

A woman's thighs in vintage hose.

2

My earliest memory, though some doubt it,

Came from when I was six months old:

A deathly cough; I felt I floated

Mid-air, though knowing I was held

In someone's arms, for sure my mother.

My sight unformed, I glimpsed another

Figure observe me anxiously,

The kitchen dark to me, but grey

That shape, surely my Auntie Cecie.

At six months I had whooping cough;

Dimly I was aware of love

Willing the desperate cough to ease. I

Saw grey too from the window pane.

Mum fought for me: I breathed again.

3

I'm certain that I never viewed her

Naked, her nighties always fleece;

No snapshots from her youth were ruder

Than in a bathing suit, one-piece;

I wasn't breastfed; my first sight of

Bare breasts were Sheba's, at a height of

Ten thousand feet, twin cones, snow-capped,

Drawn in a book that held me rapt,

King Solomon's Mines. Her body hidden,

My mummy's copious underwear,

Boned corset, slip, longline brassiere,

Bloomers, my seeing them not forbidden,

Are comforting images I find

In my impressionable mind.

4

Mum was approaching her mid-thirties

When I was born; had not been keen

To have a second child: one's start is

So loud, night-waking, rarely clean.

Dad used a proverb when he asked it

Of her—not all eggs in one basket—

And that convinced her, it would seem.

A later memory: the gleam

Above of the Milky Way, my father

Clutching my hand, when I was four.

I asked him was it peace or war,

And he said peace, though in a rather

Uncertain tone, for that starshine

Was in the summer of '39.

5

Much from that evening I remember,

Like hearing, earlier, from our lounge pouffe,

Dad and a pal engage in sombre

Discussion; during which, as if

The gravity of the situation

Evoked a psychic manifestation,

A huge, black, ugly thing I saw

Scurry, a longlegged Swastika,

Across our carpet, swift as lightning.

From the pouffe, unnoticed, up I jumped

And ran to intercept it, stamped

On the house-spider. It wasn't frightening,

I calmly peeled it, splayed out flat,

From my small sandal's sole, and sat.

6

My first schoolday, a rainy, blustery

Morning, my mummy dragging me,

Tearful, from comfort into mystery;

A crowded cloakroom's smell of pee

And rubbery macs. What calms my fear is

Seeing a pretty blond girl near us,

She and her mum are still, serene,

Alone in the blubbing frantic scene.

I fall for her: her classic features

Framed perfectly by her short fringed hair...

I won't mind school if she is there;

O brave new world, to have such creatures!

Alas, a whistle ends that joy—

She with the girls, I with the boys.

7

My second erotic recollection:

Aged five or six, I am in bed

One morning with a throat infection—

My parents' bed, being cosseted.

Mum had a close friend with her, Kitty;

My dad adored her, lively, pretty.

The women standing near my side

I saw, at the same moment, slide

A stocking up... knee... thigh... Elation,

At least surprise. What made me frame,

'Long stockings!' Smiles, laughter, came.

It was my first ejaculation!

Kitty: 'Long stockings, yes!' A smile,

With skirts raised, ever since beguiles.

8

My mother made our small home cosy

But didn't teach me names of plants

As Laurie Lee's did before Rosie

Showed him more riches Nature grants;

No, she was never an earth-mother,

But was, in fact, inclined to smother

Her late-born son, holding me back

From rough games, fun in a hay-stack.

Though with grey hair when I first knew her

She was still plumply beautiful,

Her fine soprano voice would thrill.

Her looks at twenty though! I'd screw her,

I've fantasised, if I had met

That roguish, tousle-black-haired *soubrette*!

I'd have received a look that freezes,

For she was staunchly Methodist

And loved her Harold more than Jesus;

Also she'd never, she confessed,

Reacted keenly to the sexual.

I can't think dad was ineffectual

In bed; I know his blood was hot;

It's probable she was just not

Inclined that way. With a clear brightness

She shone, but gave out little heat;

Unfailingly she smiled, was sweet

And kind. Dad needed Amy's lightness,

'She keeps me going,' he'd say, his jests

Belying Black Dog, a frequent guest.

10

He passed to me that vicious canine.

My antidote has been to write,

Stumble along the Muse's ley line

And nourished always by the sight

Of girls in sleek hose, elegant Cuban

Heels and straight seams; their bodies Rubens

Would have loved painting in the nude;

But I prefer the eye to brood

On the rich treasure trove revealed by

A skirt raised over the rich mesh

Of fabrics from which bursts plump flesh.

The Dog my father was assailed by

He quelled with solos and duets,

Mingled with jokes and cigarettes.

11

For jokes he knew he could rely on

His workmate Freddy, his brain slow.

'She's bleddy told a man he's dyin'!'—

A nurse had said, 'You're very low.'

Dad told it like a comedic master,

Freddy's shocked face, the colour of plaster;

'Tellin' a man he'll soon be dead!'

'She meant of course he was low in bed

And needed to be raised by pillows.'

It was dad's laughter made us all,

Family and friends, hysterical,

Coming in waves that rose to billows.

I still recall how his voice rang

In jokes, and soulfully when he sang.

12

The blackout up, an air raid looming,

I would be listening from my pouffe

As mum and dad sang 'In the Gloaming'

And other songs portraying love,

And loved their voices harmonising,

His plunging low and her voice rising,

My sister trilling on the keys.

Their songs I've kept, but no one plays.

I learned from them to sound romantic

Yet truly it was genuine,

That primal blend of *yang* and *yin.*

Their repertoire was transatlantic,

Songs brought from Broadway to Redruth,

Ballads from their Edwardian youth.

13

Born in America, teenaged Lois,

My sister, curvy, auburn-haired,

Vivacious, played with equal prowess

For a short period while she cared—

A young girl's nature being fickle—

Piano keys or hearts, a trickle

Of allied forces turning soon

To a vast host at the high noon

Of readiness for D-Day. Lois,

As pretty and bosomy as our mum,

Exploded on them like a bomb;

I sensed our parents' worry grow as

She came flush-cheeked from every dance

For she was eager for romance.

14

Bombs fell around us; we would huddle

Under our basement stairs, and made

A closeknit four, one common cuddle.

I was too young to be afraid.

Dad's whisper: 'Falmouth's getting pounded.'

Relief when at last the all-clear sounded.

Though not called up, his life was hard,

After his day's toil, the Home Guard.

Not much use if we were imperilled,

An axe he carried, not a gun.

'Bet you can use that, h'mm?—Good man!'

'What did the General say to'ee, 'Arold?'

His mates asked after the parade;

'That I was the smartest in the brigade.'

15

I broke my elbow falling over

My mother's picnic basket on

Rocky Carn Marth. I'd soon recover

After a first op badly done

At Redruth, the next day in Truro

Re-set: 'You can go home tomorrow.'

But no, a dangerous disease

Brought by someone from overseas

Meant 'quarantine'. A perplexed, fearful

Timelessness. I saw mum and dad

Gaze once through glass at me, waving, sad,

Atop a fire escape. They said my tearful

Dimly-seen face caused so much pain

They simply couldn't come again.

16

Our home, a bungalow my father

Built at weekends and after work,

Was small, we four were yoked together

Tightly, yet I would see ghosts after dark

And yelled so loud and caused such trouble

Most nights I ended in the double

Bed beside dad, my mum in mine.

Cuddling into him I felt fine,

Heat pouring out through his pyjamas

And a male smell. When pretty Pam,

An evacuee from London, came

And shared with Lois girlish dramas,

Where we all slept it's hard to know:

Five into beds for four won't go.

17

I saw pain on our parents' faces:

Lois brought home, under arrest.

She'd 'borrowed' mail, to copy phrases

She liked, expressions that impressed

Her, probably the most romantic.

The furore that it caused was frantic,

For her first job was at the Post

Office. Letters reported lost,

Then turning up. In wartime, treason!

Our parents' agony was great,

Until a kindly magistrate

Felt Lois was too young for prison.

She'd had a 'brainstorm' it was said,

Given psychiatric help instead.

18

Undoubtedly dad craved affection;

When Lois was sixteen or so

My mother and I heard from the kitchen

Lois in her bedroom shout out, 'No!

Get off!' I hear it now as clear as

The Chopin playing. Her door, near us,

Was open, so the sudden stir

Was nothing hidden, sinister,

Yet why did memory retain it?

Mum called, as if well used to this,

'Lois, just give your dad a kiss!'

Then silence fell. I can't explain it.

Lois would say he touched her breast.

She loved him dearly. Let it rest.

19

I only really noticed Lois

When she, eighteen, began to date

Yankees, who'd bring her home to show us

They could be trusted. I was eight,

Thrilled by the war—the Allies winning

Battles at last—also beginning

To take an interest, somewhat strange,

In Lois's rushing home to change

To go out dancing. I'd be seated

In our front room reading a book

By our coal fire, sneaking a look

As Lois, munching toast, completed

Her dolling up with stockings clipped

To her suspenders. I was rapt.

20

Was that the only revelation—

Her stockings clipped? It can't be so;

I'd receive laughter, acclamation,

In our home village, where we'd go

To spend with aunts and uncles Sundays.

I'd mime her movements donning undies

In 'forfeits' at a Sunday School

Social—the bra on, then the pull

And strain behind her back to fasten;

Yet it can't be I saw her tits?

And yet I had the hall in fits

As though I'd given a masterclass in

Girls dressing... Suspenders, one by one...

I thought I thought it was just fun.

21

I think I saw her arms, in weaving

Patterns around her buxom form,

As like in some ways searchlights cleaving

The black sky, keeping us from harm,

For both were equally fascinating:

Tensions; and tense too was our waiting

To see which officer would gain

Her hand in marriage; it was plain

One of them would—she found romantic

Their uniforms, peaked caps and Wings,

The glamour young male courage brings.

Her love life drove our parents frantic:

What if someone broke through *before*?...

I was a child of Love and War.

22

Also, by eight, I was a General.

'Books for our troops' had begged my school.

Dad gave me, with a quiet valour, all

He had to give, a cupboardful

Of the world's mysteries he valued—

I saw his loss as he hard-swallowed—

National Geographic magazines.

These were his dreams, his unseen scenes.

The Head thought *their* needs were more urgent

And kept them in the school, being wise.

I honour my dad's sacrifice;

For three books I'd have been a sergeant;

For these, like riches from the Raj,

I proudly wore a General's badge.

23

At home, being shy, I watched in silence,

Observed, as future writers do;

Liked Captain Skadden, who brought nylons

For mum and Lois, a shimmering new

Invention, so fine, almost transparent.

Luckies for dad came in a torrent,

To me, a baseball bat and ball.

Jimmy was Texan, craggy, tall.

Mum and dad worried: ten years older

Than Lois, he might well be wed,

Or taken floozies to his bed;

What scandals might be in his folder?

Already they'd two offspring planned

While smooching to Glen Miller's band.

24

Long before Jimmy and Glenn Miller

Our home was half-American,

We had our 'breakfast nook' and 'cooler',

For under Californian sun

My parents lived in their prime twenties,

It was their golden age of plenty;

I'd gaze at albums full of snaps,

Dad and a brother, snazzy chaps,

And mum chic, lovely as Jean Harlow;

My dad especially could seem

Caught up in his American Dream,

Almost on an extended furlough

From Beverly Hills, Los Angeles,

So made the G.I.s feel at ease.

25

Lessening the chance she'd 'get in trouble'

Dad let them dance in our front room.

Yet Lois played a kind of double

Love game: the American at home,

Away, an Australian navigator,

Insurance possibly for later.

Passionate kisses in our porch,

Then under bedclothes with a torch

She'd write two letters, one to Jimmy

To give him the next day—he had

To write her too, their love quite mad—

Then she would scribble a less steamy

'Bluey' to Ray, bombing somewhere:

'Blueys'—slim letters light as air.

26

Three years before, when fog had grounded

All flights, they'd dated for nine days;

He'd watched her at a dance, surrounded

By suitors, but she'd caught his gaze.

Dad would recall how he had seen them

With 'not a coat of paint' between them,

Strolling; he'd stopped his van and glared,

Feeling his daughter unprepared

At sixteen for such close encounters.

But for the next three years they wrote,

And from the paragraphs she'd quote

He was not one of the skirt-hunters

But serious, a Methodist—

And young, untouched; he passed that test.

27

And yet, and yet, she could remember

Him short, she thought; she'd have to change

Her shoes... He might have been an ember

Slow-fading in our Cornish Range

For she and Jimmy loved so madly.

She'd look back at this moment sadly—

Seeing his messenger alight

With a short note: 'Can't come tonight'.

Next day the quiet road outside our

Home was jammed tight with vehicles,

Khaki trucks, jeeps, bound for the Fal's

Beaches. Death was the lead Rider,

Behind whom G.I.s threw us gum.

The queue was endless, struck us dumb.

28

While they in Normandy were fighting

A colour photo came from Ray:

Sweet face, and its peaked cap delighting

Lois; and I, though God knows why,

Said he looked nice. His features shaded

Softly together, he enfiladed

Jimmy's position with one shot.

God knows what Lois truly thought,

Confused, divided. Then her mother

Said, 'Lois, dear, he is the one!'

Lois wrote Jimmy a 'Dear John';

Days later, tearful, wrote another:

'I didn't mean it! I love *you*!'

Wounded, shipped home, he never knew.

29

With her lot cast, the air of tension

Ebbed from our home. Lois would blame

Her mother for her intervention

Over her marriage choice, but came

To accept fate. I'm sure I missed it,

The tension I hadn't known existed

Until I felt it fade to calm,

Lois no longer rushing home

And finishing by the fire her dressing

To rush out. I oiled my cricket bat,

Poor Jimmy's baseball bat forgot.

Whether those years were curse or blessing

Their influence on me is immense:

I liked things—war, clothes, women—tense.

30

A pal and I, each an Eleven,

Played long Test matches in the field

Behind my home, the ground uneven,

Cowpatted. Once, mum came out, called,

'Time to come in!' The day was glooming,

But victory for my team was looming:

I shouted, 'Fuck!' though God knows how,

I'd picked the word up, didn't know

Its meaning. Her face red and furious,

She sent me to bed, at six o'clock.

I lay there, thinking about fuck,

Simply a word, yet somehow serious.

Then dad came home. They talked, I guess,

And I was mildly told to dress.

31

I'm sure Freud would have discovered plenty

Had he explored our simple house

As tension-packed as G. A. Henty,

A writer I found marvellous,

Almost as great as Rider Haggard.

In sexual knowledge I was laggard,

An unknown land as far away

As Australia, Lois's destiny.

'There are four people,' wrote the master,

'In every coitus.' I agree,

At least it's very true of me.

The palace of Oedipus and Jocasta

Had nothing on our tiny house,

And still now 'There are four of us'.

32

I loved our Saturdays: first, rugby,

Watching the 'Reds', then after that

The pictures: smoky darkness, snug by

My dad; the screen was often at

The midpoint of a sultry drama;

No matter, it was Hollywood glamour

And tension, the stars smoking too.

With comedies, pals always knew—

'I 'eard 'ee at the Regal, 'Arold!'—

When he was there, from his huge laugh

That set the entire audience off.

Then waiting for the *Football Herald*,

Pacing the platform for the train,

So we could live the match again.

33

Ray had sailed here and left with 'Bluey';

Then Bluey's blueys to us were

So racked with homesickness all through we

Decided we would follow her.

An American Minister uncle, Willie,

Visiting, drew sketches I thought silly

To show me what sex was about.

What's sex?... Mum and dad were out,

They'd left it to this former miner

To show how penises can extend,

Thicken and harden so they end

In holes that wives had, the vagina.

I felt disgust. My parents came

Late home, in their expressions shame.

34

We were just crossing the equator,

I in the ship's library

In long shorts and a thick wool sweater

Worn, though the heat was killing me,

To hide my bulk, I thought. While browsing,

By chance I found a page so rousing,

'Roseate nipples... luscious breasts'

Being played with, not like Sheba's crests,

But warm and girlish. Of a sudden

I felt a stir, a lovely ache,

A force through all my body wake,

My cock become enormous, harden,

Straining against my shorts. It cried

For more, its red knob poked outside.

35

I had to wait till it subsided

Before I faced the atrocious heat.

Strange, that where hemispheres collided

Childhood and puberty chose to meet.

I saw dad deckchaired, reading specs on,

Couldn't imagine his erection.

At night new stars, the Southern Cross,

But he and I both felt the loss

Of Cornwall, even in midwinter.

Shipboard, no further hard-ons came,

But life would never be the same

Again, I sensed, for it would centre

On what for grown-ups replaced toys,

The dolphin-leap that brought brief joy.

Two

Dreamtime

1

And so, mid ocean and mid world,

My nine to fourteen neutered spell

Ceased, and I was abruptly hurled

Into that heaven and that hell,

Sex that now calms the soul, now rages.

I find, in the four hundred pages

Of Howard Spring's *My Son, My Son*

That gifted me my first hard-on,

I'd stumbled on the only passage

That was erotic—timidly,

But powerful enough for me.

My soul had flashed to me a message:

It is high time, my son, my son,

Your days of ignorance were gone!

2

In Melbourne we were reconvening,

The primal four of us, plus Ray;

I spent my early months there keening

For Cornwall, but we had to stay

Two years or else refund the money

For our ten-pounds-a-person journey.

We lived in a three bedroom flat.

At once it was apparent that

My room was full of ghosts and spiders,

Enormous ones, tarantulas

So-called, although not poisonous.

Mum and I were again night gliders,

She flitting to my haunted bed

And I, at fourteen, couched by dad.

3

Ray, short, stocky, somewhat a let-down

To Lois, in his height at least,

Since half our bomber crews were shot down

A hero therefore, never ceased

To rile me, for I found him bossy,

Bumptious and loud, a cocky Aussie.

One night I was outside their room

Quietly creeping to turf out mum;

He burst out suddenly, bollock-naked,

All hairy sweat, his large dong swung,

A snarling ape, a short King Kong;

What could I say? I had to fake it:

'I'm going to fetch that *Photoplay*.'

He shoved past to shower sex away.

4

I didn't think sex in the moment,

Being still utterly naïve,

Could not conceive his sudden show meant

That mysterious act—though I believe

The smells from sex are rather splendid

And should be slept with. That shock ended

My nights of breathing dad's hot fumes—

My parents deciding we'd switch rooms;

They would take mine, its ghosts and spiders,

And I theirs, dad no doubt pissed off

With lack of sex; they called my bluff;

I found now far more long-legged sliders

Entering, through a jungly tree

To open window then to me.

5

After the sounds of late night bustle,

Deep silence falling, I would lie

In terror, hearing the tree rustle;

I'd leave the light on, keep one eye

Open to catch black legs appearing;

Sweat drenched me, for the heat was wearing;

Mosquitos whined. Those awful nights!

Brief drowses when God knows what sights

Appeared—I'd wake to my prick humping

Some succubus, a sticky wet

White stuff now mixing with the sweat.

And yet the feel of my prick pumping

Did not encourage or provoke

My hand, at any time, to stroke.

6

Of course I had no sexual tutor,

An older brother, say, or chum,

No ready porn on a computer,

Showing how hands can make you come;

Knowing no way to instant pleasure

I had to ease the throbbing pressure

Through poetry and music, fate

Compelling me to sublimate.

Yet still, considering I was clever,

And had erections like a rod,

My blindness in this sphere was odd.

One wonders if my mummy ever

Observed me touch and made it plain

She'd cut it off if touched again.

7

At school my class was studious, quiet,

All boys alas still, mostly Jews.

Classes back home had been a riot,

Boys with one purpose, to confuse

The masters, mock them, rile them, madden.

Our R.I. teacher, Mr Hadden,

His efforts to keep order dire,

We'd greet by standing like a choir

And sing a chorus from *Messiah*.

Being Cornish we could sing quite well,

In harmony. My Aussie school

Had standards altogether higher.

Although in time this would bear fruit

I loathed my double-breasted suit.

8

I felt choked by it as I sat in

My first class with a woman, young

And pretty, there to teach us Latin.

She found the new, fat boy among

Familiar forms, and with a pleasant

Smile asked my name. A downtrod peasant

Still, I said 'Thomas'. Then she said,

'Can I call you Tom?' This quickly led

Through mumbled words to her addressing

Me, not even as Donald, but as Don.

Happier with it from that day on

I see Miss Gordon as a blessing;

She had that lovely gift, too rare

In teachers I had known—to care.

9

After I'd bragged about my cricket

My class chose me as opening bat;

The second ball knocked back the wicket;

They didn't pick me after that,

But didn't mock me or turn ratty

Nor shame me with the nickname 'Fatty'

As boys had done at my old school;

These were all decent boys, not cruel.

But life was simply a procession

Between our flat and Uni High;

Dreams might be wet but days were dry,

I had no focus for obsession;

Having to fall back on myself

I raided Lois's bookshelf.

10

Her book club choices were light fiction.

I chose *The Haunting of Toby Jugg*;

It magnified my night-affliction

And yet I craved it like a drug.

He, paralysed, deprived of motion,

Hears in the dark a soft commotion

And realises it's a swarm

Of spiders; they scurry over him.

His torture's climax is the Mother

Of all spiders, when the moon is full,

Monstrous above his window sill,

Plopping in, huge enough to smother

My *alter ego* in his bed.

That Mother-spider crazed my head.

11

One Sunday I was reading after

Our usual roast, sprawled in my room;

Then from the next-door lounge came laughter;

I broke from Jugg's delirium

Or from some text-book too long studied,

Got up and went to the sun-flooded

Lounge. I observed, quite near the door,

My sister lying on the floor,

Kicking her legs up high, while side-on

To her, behind, the others gazed

At her contortions, amused, amazed;

A mid-air bike she seemed to ride on,

Flat on her back; I gathered that

Her object was to burn off fat.

12

While pedalling she was chuckling, grunting,

Just as amused as dad, mum, Ray;

I halted where I was confronting

Her swirling feet. The mood was gay,

I chuckling too. But what was hidden

Was tumult, for her skirt had ridden

To waist height; right before my eyes,

Head-on, were her plump, sweaty thighs

Bursting out of her nylons, tensely

Stretched by thick black suspender straps;

Sunlight made gleam their clasps and clips,

And what completed it—immensely,

Between those thighs, her gusset bulged;

Few brothers were ever more indulged.

13

Her panties, I believe, were black and

The gusset sweated; each side, hairs

Escaped; her pedalling never slackened,

She seemed oblivious to my stares.

I've learned the tribe who rose and sank there

Had a dark word for it—her *dung-ka*,

Sounding much like my sister's grunts.

As unknown to me then was *cunt*,

Our word, but I saw the Mother-spider

In a benign way, for it begged

Comparison, from the swirl of legs,

The black suspenders stretched each side her

All-powerful centre. I also saw

A kind of whirling Swastika.

14

Timeless, for they were so entrancing;

Those moments fixed my taste for life,

Before my gaze that image dancing

When choosing a brief love or wife:

Thighs after face—are they too slender

To complement and strain suspenders?

My childish cry, 'Long stockings!' were

A signal and early harbinger.

I went on staring, her legs churning,

And both continue to this day.

But then, from chuckling also, Ray

Ended the floor show without warning,

Snarling, **'Shoo! Shoo! Go to your room!'**

It startled like a sonic boom.

15

That vision and his harsh reaction

Fought in me, sprawling on my bed.

I guess he spotted an erection,

Something I hadn't known I had

In my enchantment. I resented

The unfairness: for he seemed contented

For dad to stay there, though I grant

That he was watching her aslant.

Still, Ray was out of line and pettish

I still believe, unworthy of

A drama so wonderful and grave,

The dawning of a lifelong fetish.

Not that I knew it then, that strange

Magic, only that I was changed.

16

'Changed utterly'—to quote a favourite

Poet; 'a terrible beauty is born.'

I found a way that I could savour it,

Through the equivalent of porn

Seen daily by the most respectable

People in Melbourne: quite delectable

Females in corsets, girdles, bras,

Completely inoffensive as

They were just sketched—but realistic,

Those adverts clearly drawn with love;

In sexiness they were far above

Today's hardcore. Carnal yet mystic,

They adorned *The Age*, Ray's newspaper;

This was what women wore—and were.

17

A different breed, and almost species

From now; I loved the matronly

Models, stern-corseted and gracious,

And the young maidens, lyrically

Displayed in bras and girdles, lither;

I'd get a hard-on seeing either.

They also comforted, in some obscure

Way—'foundations' sounds so sure.

Elsewhere were ads for hats, gloves, dresses;

It was the age of elegance,

The New Look of Dior from France,

And what a woman wears expresses

Her soul. They liked being feminine,

'Supported', sitting with care, held in.

18

So long as it was gripped to stockings,

Corset or girdle got me hard,

There had to be that interlocking.

But still, amazingly, I was barred

From jerking off. There were no other

Females in my life apart from mother

And sister. Sometimes on the tram

During my afternoon ride home

There'd be green-blazered girls strap-hanging,

I'd see their white-bloused bosoms strain,

And have such hard-ons there'd be pain

Mixed with unutterable longing;

Slowly the former would abate

Along our road in the fierce heat.

19

I loved film stars, bullet-bra sweatered

Above cinched waists, in dramas or

Hollywood musicals, never bettered,

In their released joy after war,

For brilliant lyrics and romantic

Songs. With too sober or pedantic

Friends I still love to break the spell

By warbling songs from *Carousel*.

They stare as if I've lost my reason.

But in my teens the music played

Support role to the female lead,

Say, Doris Day or Kathryn Grayson.

In age the music cheers and heals

Better than antidepressant pills.

20

I wrote my first erotic story,

I'm rather sorry it's been lost,

My pleasure in it transitory—

Lois exposed it at Sunday roast,

Princess Margaret and I were petting,

A cinema back row our setting.

She brandished it, quoted. Red from shame

I fled to my room. Soon Lois came,

Waving a book about English gardens,

Smiling said, 'Donald, you write like this!

Nice things!' I've given nice a miss.

At least it was girls induced my hard-ons;

Beverley Nichols, I learn, was queer,

Which might have spoiled his book for her.

21

One day, I don't know why, I entered

Her room, and was shocked to find her there,

Dressing. At once my gaze was centred

Upon her notch of pubic hair,

The slip or frock with which she fumbled

Trapping her head and bust. I mumbled

And fled. That burning bush still shone.

She came to me: 'Has anyone

Told you about sex?' Kind eyes went through me.

I answered, 'Yes.' She nodded, left.

I lay in turbulence, bereft,

And recall thinking, 'You ought to *show* me!'

It was the only time I caught

An openly incestuous thought.

22

I thrilled to pop, *'You are temptation*

And I am yours!' Sprawled in my room

All evening. Heard on a Classics station,

Night after night, in gathering gloom,

The first dark chords of a concerto,

Rachmaninov's. Still didn't dare to

Turn off the light till dawn was there.

Lusted at the foundation wear

Of portly mother figures, dreamier

Young girls, one advert with a quote

Which seemed, like the girdled girl, to float—

About a queen who'd ruled Bohemia:

'Tell me if she were not design'd

Th'eclipse and glory of mankind?'

23

I realised my isolation,

My hunger—simply—for a friend

From the other half in all creation,

One afternoon when, at the end

Of an exam, I trudged, hot, lonely,

To the school tram stop. There was only

One other waiting there, so cool

In her green blazer, beautiful.

My heart turned over. How I longed to

Address her: but what would I say?

She scarcely looked, face turned away.

Then to the world that she belonged to

A tram, not mine, carried her off,

Leaving me with a hopeless love.

24

A raging love, and epiphanic,

So sweet her short and straight blonde hair,

Her cool fair face. Amidst the panic

Of first school, ten years earlier,

I'd seen a girl with her complexion

And hair, and the same calm reaction,

Lovely, and that had quenched my tears

At leaving mummy. Now, ten years

On, was she *that* infant, for so many

Had sailed to find the Southern Cross?

I'd felt, more briefly and mildly, loss,

As that school also baulked at any

Mingling of sexes. Improbable,

But those two visions haunt me still.

25

Lois and Ray worked in the city,

Dad with a building gang, and mum,

For extra money in the kitty—

Each week they sent food parcels home—

At a nearby factory, rather drolly

Making what I considered holy,

Nylons. Each morning separately

We left, and the last one put the key

Under a stone. One day I lingered,

Hidden from view in our back lane,

Then, the time ripe, stole in again:

I'd find the girl for whom I hungered,

At least *a* girl of flesh and blood,

Making the best of what I had.

26

I roamed the flat, its silent starkness.

Our landlady, who lived beneath

On the ground floor, always in darkness,

Was old, reclusive, still as death.

Then I undressed; to my great pleasure

We'd moved from wool suit to green blazer.

Everything came off. Then I cased

Lois's room, cool, scented, chaste.

I walked around it like its master.

Opened a drawer: a tangled mesh

Of wispy nylons, scented, fresh.

Opened another; heart beat faster—

Bras and suspender belts, roll on.

Then slowly Donna replaced Don.

27

I applied lipstick and eye shadow;

Couldn't wear shoes nor change my hair;

Mirrored, I was no Brigitte Bardot

But loved this friend I'd fashioned. Fear

Augmented greatly my excitement:

Each sound I heard, however slight, meant

Someone's return. I loved the pull

Of the suspenders, my thighs cool,

As I walked around, and the elastic

Roll on trapping my stiff prick tight,

So that on looking down I might

Be all-girl. The tingle was fantastic.

There was no rush; hushed hours... At four

Mum came, when I was Don once more.

28

Day followed day; I craved more terror,

So much my pleasure it increased;

I had to bring discovery nearer,

Wanted to be observed crossdressed.

I wasn't sure if she should see or

Only hear swish my quasi-Dior

Skirt—the sole other in the house,

The crone who never bothered us.

Stairs down to deep murk I descended,

Heart pounding—would there be a tryst?

A tingle—small spider on my wrist;

I cried out, shook it off. That ended

My craze; as swiftly as my tight

Skirt let me I fled up to light.

29

My dad, who toiled in broiling heat and

The winter's chill, at a hospital,

Scaffolded sky-high, his hard life sweetened

By—God knows, nothing much at all,

Missing the place of his upbringing,

His siblings, the after-chapel singing—

Came home that day, his mood sky-high,

And told us over supper why:

Plastering outside in sultry weather

He'd glanced into a ward and seen

A patient sponge her breasts, serene,

Attractive; they'd smiled at one another;

She went on sponging. I was glad

That generous woman thrilled my dad.

30

Of course I was also slightly jealous:

A woman smiling while exposed!

It was quite bold of him to tell us.

Next day, when I'd unlocked and closed

The door, that scene was still onturning.

I didn't strip at once that morning,

I clomped around, I was not rushed;

But finally I went and pushed

Open her door... Froze to a statue:

Lois was in bed bolt-upright,

Eyes bulging from her face, chalk-white.

'Donald, it's you! Thank God! I thought you

Were a rapist, such a heavy tread!'

A cold had kept her home in bed.

31

I can't recall my explanation;

Unhappy, probably, at school.

Lois's fear of violation

She would narrate in such a droll

Way that it brought on gales of laughter

That suppertime and many after.

It was the end of our affair—

I stole into her room no more.

But there was still, of course, a moiety

Of all I saw of womanhood,

A woman of my flesh and blood

Who could provide variety,

Foundations of a different age

Familiar from my infant stage.

32

It's possible that my erotic

Filial union came before

The fraternal union, more theatric;

Certainly this was easier,

I only had to wait till nightfall.

When mum and dad gave up their rightful

Bedroom to me, they could not find

Space in their room, so left behind

The wardrobe and the chest of drawers.

At leisure then I could explore

Mum's hosiery and underwear,

Pink corset, patterned with bright flowers,

Stiffened with whalebone stays, a vast

Garment that breathed our Cornish past.

33

The window tree, the sky's light fading,

Was jungly, jagged-leaved, its hordes

Of vast tarantulas bent on raiding,

Matched by Rachmaninov's sombre chords,

Preceded by *'You are temptation*

And I am yours...' on the pop station;

I lying hidden by a sheet,

Throbbing too, longing to complete

Something unknown except in dreaming.

Faintly came Lois's *Rustle of Spring*

On the piano, signalling

Long hours of dread before redeeming

Dawn light. Before that roseate dawn

My mother-lover had long gone.

34

One night she came in, a bright smile on

Her face—I was sprawled out in bed—

Then stiffened, as she saw two nyloned

Feet sticking out. Feebly I said,

In answer to her obvious query,

'Why are you wearing those, dear?' 'I

Was feeling cold.' Was that a sly

Smile she afforded fleetingly?

I'm only certain that she nodded,

Both of us broiling, bathed in sweat,

And left with the clothes she'd come to get.

A lesser woman would have prodded,

But mum showed not the least surprise:

A village woman, simple, wise.

35

What seems to me rather surprising:

While I was being so perverse,

My mental faculties were rising,

When one might anticipate the reverse.

That Australian sojourn was my Dreamtime,

Eros and Psyche at the same time

Growing. A film, *The Blue Lagoon*,

Quoted a poem by John Donne;

I found it later, *The Good Morrow*;

'Were we not wean'd till then, but suck'd

On country pleasures?...' I was struck

By poetry as by an arrow.

I thought, That's passion! and one day

With good luck it will come my way.

36

I read all Ray's *Roget's Thesaurus*

While bored in long vacation blues,

My mind to knowledge wholly porous.

I started reading book reviews,

Asked for and devoured a novel

About Rumanians crushed by evil

Nazi and Stalinist regimes.

I loved its serious, sombre themes.

But also... In solitary confinement,

Cold rising from the concrete floor,

A woman we have known before

As being all middleclass refinement

Finds that she needs to urinate,

It matters more than love or hate.

37

She shouts and bangs, but no one answers;

So squats and feels—I'd never read

The like in Lois's romances—

'Blisfully the warm wet spread

Through her suspender belt, her stockings...'

So realistic and so shocking;

I realised it affected me

In different ways, conflictingly.

I have since wondered if the writer

Also had complex feelings there;

The creative mind is saint and whore.

I'd find the greater Russians later,

But *The Twenty-fifth Hour* was where I cast

Off childish things: 'the hour after the last'.

38

It felt like that—too late—when Sara

And other girls were suddenly

Part of my class. There's nothing clearer

In all my Melbourne history

Than seeing, from the desk I sat in,

Her short black hair, pale nape, in Latin,

So close they might have felt my breath,

Unless it's when, in our *Macbeth*

Class read-around, I heard her utter,

'Come to my woman's breasts!' I fell

For her, she walked on asphodel;

Was she in hose? It didn't matter,

She had such slim, light-footed grace,

Such a sweet, open, tender face!

39

More than *Macbeth* for me in tragic

Power was the knowledge I must lose

Almost at once this late-found magic.

I'd beaten all the clever Jews

In class exams, I was delirious

From my first love—none is more serious,

Loved girls around, their fresh perfume,

But soon we would be travelling home,

The home for which I'd long been grieving.

But now I wept at Sunday roast.

I spoke to Sara on my last

Day—'I just want to say I'm leaving.'

Puzzled—she scarcely knew this *goy*—

She shook my hand and moved away.

Three

In marriage and Windermere

1

'You've lovely legs!' observed my father,

Smiling, when I had introduced

My first girlfriend. (Maureen was rather

Charmed by his words.) 'You choose your first

Wife,' my old friend Elena reckoned,

Puffing *Sobranie*, 'but your second'—

She was a second—'chooses you.'

In my case I think neither true.

My marriage to Maureen was chosen

By custom: we had gone to bed

Together, therefore we should wed,

For both of us our futures frozen.

My second wife I chose, though one

Could argue it was Ross, our son.

2

None of that's accurate, not wholly,

For work I'd have to move away

And was not fit to survive solely;

Maureen was smart and housewifely,

Could bake already a good pasty,

Had Cornish wit, dry but not nasty,

We were both workingclass, I shy

With girls, posh ones especially...

All that, besides its being expected.

As for Denise, those ten years on,

I feel, from an initial sign,

By destiny we were elected

To marry. It was strange, the way

I addressed her on a humdrum day...

3

'You've lovely legs!' I called out, smiling.

Long, shapely, nyloned legs on broad

Stairs—the legs first, therefore beguiling,

She first down, so I could afford

To offer my young unmet student

Spontaneous praise, albeit imprudent,

Almost before her face appeared.

Clatter, as her co-students cleared

The upstairs classroom and descended.

Denise smiled, as Maureen had done

When dad, in the same courteous tone,

Had said those words. Some power intended

Both marriages; how else would I

Have echoed him spontaneously?

4

I must go back to our homecoming:

We've moved a long way down the track.

The family house now, without plumbing,

A cobwebbed privy round the back;

Large house that faded elegantly,

Uncles and aunts who faded gently,

All three with quiet, loving souls

Who played on sunny Sundays bowls

On our smooth lawn before the service

Mainly enjoyed for the sweet hymns.

I hear them still as the light dims.

'St. Martin's Villa' I would love as

For Sara I grew less forlorn:

The house where dad and I were born.

5

I liked the ageing village people,

Poor, for the mines around were dead;

Two-up two-downs, below the chapel

And us, held everything they had.

Back gardens all along the terrace

Below us raised a frenzied chorus

Of sheets being beaten on the lines

And chatter—weddings, piles, chilblains,

A broken pipe, or heart, or cooker,

On Monday mornings, in Carnkie.

I liked the life and, school done, I

Walked to the Institute for snooker;

All male still, but a cosy club,

Only alternative to the pub.

6

My family shunned the booze as lethal,

Had known the misery it spread.

My aunts in cameos: oldest, Ethel,

Lived with us later. Daughters dead,

Heavy in heart and body—D-cups.

Cecie would never fill the teacups,

Rushing too much; would always run,

Taking to sick folk 'a few yeast buns'.

A heart of gold. Nellie, staid, gentle,

Still wore the ring her fiancé

Gave her: the Somme swept him away.

At Christmas donned a gypsy's mantle

And wobbly teeth to make us laugh;

Recited grandly Kipling's *If*.

7

Our uncle Eddie, after Cecie

Had given him breakfast and then tied

His laces, rested, took it easy,

Watched the unchanging carn outside

With *Readers' Digest*, pipe and matches;

Moved from the window in rare snatches

To practise mum and dad's duet

Accompaniments. I tried to get

Him novels, but he didn't care for

What wasn't real. Had lost his spouse

Early to TB. He was humorous,

Twinkly-eyed, wise, a true gent, therefore

Much loved by all. He had a son

Cecie had raised as though her own.

8

A relative by marriage, cap'n

Of one of the tin mines, had left

Them the house unwillingly, as can happen

When couples of offspring are bereft.

It gave to us a *Cherry Orchard*

Flavour—except no one was tortured

By guilt, or some obscure amour,

And were, like all around, piss-poor,

On pensions, helped now by dad's earnings

From sheer hard labour, laying bricks;

His kin, I think, had outlived sex.

But really, I can't say what yearnings

Still troubled them; I only know

They let life calmly, sweetly flow.

9

Mum told an honorific auntie,

'No, Donald is always studyin',

No time for girls.'—her knowledge scanty

Regarding the Don's life within.

It's true I had a thirst for knowledge,

Which led eventually to New College

Oxford awarding me a place,

And Shelley, Hardy, Keats, I guess

Gave me less time for agonising.

I'd throb, when reading on Carn Brea,

Of Tess reclining in the hay,

But don't remember my cock rising

From any picture, any scene,

For two years, sixteen to eighteen.

10

Yet desire ached. This still distresses:

Few in the cinema and yet

A girl came and sat next, her tresses

Long and raven, a cigarette

Almost at once between her fingers.

The sensual bliss thereafter lingers—

Her face, dark, pretty, in the dusk

Came close, and a sharp scent of musk,

As her hair brushed me. I was drowning

In girlness, wholly overwhelmed.

Ronald, on my other side, becalmed,

Eyes fixed on Lou Costello clowning:

A village pal, not very bright.

The girl asked did I have a light.

11

Of course I didn't; it didn't faze her,

She was now almost in my lap,

How easy lightly to embrace her,

To fall into that tender trap,

My sexual life no longer barren.

She asked if I knew there was a fair on,

And would I like to go? O Christ,

I longed to, but this much sufficed

For now; besides, the clock hands fleeting,

It was almost time for our bus home;

Mum would be fraught if I didn't come;

Instead, I proposed to her a meeting

In a week's time, a different town;

She said yes; I shuffled out with Ron.

12

Why did I make the Regal Redruth our

Moot point, not the Kings Camborne, so

Putting her to expense and bother?

I've racked my brains but I don't know.

The days had never passed as slowly,

Interest in learning vanished wholly.

The time came; in delirium

I waited. Of course she didn't come.

Then I was even more demented;

Madly I caught the bus to where

We'd met, spent there a further hour,

And then a lifetime being haunted

By the unknown, the might-have-been;

Recalling her, I still feel pain.

13

Two years go by. The only passion

I can acknowledge, literature.

On army service, I learn Russian,

Still shy, naïve, sex-craving, pure.

On leave, I'm learning Olde Tyme dances,

A girl says yes to my shy advances,

Then stands me up at our first date.

Apologises rather late,

Only because, I find out later,

Her mum, a kindly Christian, knows

And likes my family; she throws

A fit. So was our marriage-broker fate or

Her mum is the question that it begs;

And dad was right, she'd lovely legs.

14

I've missed out several most unpleasant

Weeks being drilled on how to fight,

Eased only by dad's loving presence

In letters—he wrote every night.

I loathed the barrack's rank aromas.

Our bombardier barked, 'Say fuck, Thomas,

Or you're not going out on the piss!'

'I won't'—to stay in seemed like bliss,

Freed from the squaddies' foulmouthed racket

For one night. He would not let go,

In rapid salvos, 'Say fuck!' 'No.'

At last he turned away: 'Oh, fuck it,

Fuck off!'... A runner, panting, hoarse:

'Gunner Thomas to the Russian Course.'

15

Maureen was pretty, a sixth former

With light-brown hair and rosebud lips,

Friendly and lively—a real charmer

With a nice curve from breasts to hips.

I felt my emotional life transforming;

We held hands for a while then, warming,

First kisses, which were wonderful.

I helped her with her work at school,

An exercise in verse translation

From French. Her teacher marked it 'B',

Viewing its skill suspiciously,

But let it pass on this occasion.

The male Head caned bad girls, their skirts

Yanked up, would say, 'It's *me* this hurts.'

16

A moment in my life most thrilling:

While kissing passionately I felt,

Not knowing if she would be willing,

Her stockinged thigh up to the welt;

As touch on skin and smooth threads mingled

Somehow my wristwatch got entangled

In her suspender strap. To free

The watch and whole hand, clumsily,

Must tell her I had reached suspenders,

Surely she'd push away my hand

Angrily. No! She didn't mind!

Of all the feminine surrenders

I have experienced, none surpassed

In thrillingness that one, the first.

17

The joys of 1950s petting!

Skirts and stiff half slips yielding to

That mix of 'far enough' and letting

Hands stroke soft inner thighs then through

Into the moist and tender haven,

All the while mouths entwined. And even

If you were not allowed that far

You could feel rather *wunderbar*

From having reached suspenders, stroking

All round them the warm, tender flesh,

Sleek nylon tensely strained—the mesh

That thrilled you, while her touch, provoking,

Was on your thigh, then clothed, your cock!

Who'd prefer jeans, the zipless fuck?

18

I was profoundly in love, and proud to

Be seen with her. She was approved

By all my family; we were allowed to

Stay in, while the adults removed

With smiles and winks to Sunday chapel.

In summer, outside, a lyric dapple,

Fields, rocky carn and ruined bal,

Faintly hymnsinging's rise and fall;

Inside, whatever Maureen grants me,

She in my arms on our settee,

A finger in her was ecstasy;

Then when we hear (the sound still haunts me)

The choir's sweet (Mendelssohn's) *Lord's Prayer*

We straighten up and comb our hair.

19

This was my landscape. All around us

Grey ruins stretching up two carns.

These, and John Wesley's teaching, bound us

As one, for which my heart still yearns,

A world as fixed, though small, as Dante's,

The village folk my uncles, aunties,

All honorific. I felt guilt;

Forefathers mined, my father built.

And I? If I could make it happen

I might build also, but in verse,

And mine, go deep—without the curse

Of darkness, death, just a 'grass cap'n',

Their term for those who were employed

Above, who air and light enjoyed.

20

Despite the on-leave gratification

I still, at nineteen, couldn't wank;

For that belated revelation

I have a German star to thank.

I watched, off-duty, *The Blue Angel*,

A film, I've found, that doesn't age well,

But when I first saw Dietrich

Vamp in suspenders—black—my prick,

At every hip-sway of the strumpet

Straining against my trousers, bunched,

Frotting it—suddenly I was drenched.

I thought, good grief, a hand could pump it!

Ignored thereafter our word-list

Po-russki, almost strained my wrist.

21

I booked, at home, a seaside weekend;

I think we and our parents knew

This was the time when full sex beckoned.

Our rooms were, from that point of view,

Ideal—adjoining, isolated.

By a full moon illuminated

We lay; at first she'd only touch;

Best not to press, I thought, too much,

Went to my bed. I heard the ocean

Plash faintly, faintly too her call to me.

I entered her so easily

Yet with a turbulent emotion,

It really wasn't hard at all!

And was entirely beautiful.

22

And then, to the delight of mothers,

A ring. Dad asked me, 'Are you sure?

You're going to Oxford, you'll meet others.'

'I'm certain.' 'Then we'll say no more.'

So Oxford came, with its infinity

Of spires, gowns, bikes; and every Trinity

Term I would have my fiancée

Lodge for a week nearby. We lay

In the lush grass of Christchurch Meadow,

Lovemaking, always taking care.

Vacations more than half the year,

And there was not, so far, the shadow

My dad had warned of: I might dream

Of girls, but saw so few of them.

23

In my first year there I was sharing

Rooms with a whimsical young man;

It proved to be a pleasant pairing;

Slight, thin-bearded, Lawrentian,

He burst in once, his eyes a satyr's,

Saying he'd let me see this later—

Spick, a small girlie-magazine

That had a sister mag called *Span*.

Bill didn't last—a failing mark in

Prelims, but has my gratitude

For leading me to never-nude

Girls in the mags that Philip Larkin

Would bike through snow, in Hull, to buy:

Just smiling girls, their skirts raised high.

24

I studied hard, then loved homecoming;

Late lie-ins, snooker after tea;

Maureen then, after brisk hill-climbing;

Late back home, leaving possibly

My signature on her white Rago

Girdle. Devouring then *Zhivago*

Besides a sandwich made by mum.

Zhivago left, like a perfume,

Its trace upon my later writing;

I found it magical, its blend

Of prose and verse. Vacation end's

Stomach knot. Once, I alighting

To change, a girl bound for Bordeaux

Leaned out: 'Wish you were coming too!'

25

The desk girl at the Radcliffe Camera,

Tall as a Parthenon caryatid,

Must have thought who's this gulping stammerer

Before her as she raised her head.

Like Baudelaire's *La Géante*, full-bodied,

She'd mesmerised me as I studied:

Those buxom hips, large breasts outthrust...

I'd gazed for weeks, shaking with lust.

I couldn't... but I'd learned with sorrow

Regret burns deadlier than remorse;

I'm lifted by some psychic force:

'Would you have tea with me tomorrow?'

I could take no without distress:

I'd tried. She shocked me, saying 'Yes'.

26

I walked on air, fanfares of trumpets

Saluted me. And when she came

We had much more than tea and crumpets

To my delight. Devoid of shame

She let me stroke her all I wanted,

Then lay widespread: I was confronted

By her serene, wet, craving cunt,

A cave, befitting *La Géante.*

We could, she offered, use withdrawal

But for some reason I drew back,

It seemed enough to gaze at black

Straps straining, not to risk renewal

Of passion, this time deep inside.

She took it calmly, dignified.

27

She was by nature quiet, passive

Yet confident, with a serene

Indecency I found impressive.

She did not baulk at being seen

And heard when, having said she needed

To use my chamber pot, proceeded

To squat before me; *la Géante*

Pissed copiously like an elephant.

I was stirred, awestruck and admiring

That she'd not closed the bedroom door,

Let me observe, hear hiss and roar.

I found such openness inspiring.

Next time, she had a period;

We went to see a film instead.

28

And then I sought no more liaisons.

She was so free, warm, highly sexed,

I've racked my brain exploring reasons.

I'm sure we would if we'd had text,

Able to interchange brief greetings.

Why did I not seek further meetings?

I'd like to claim that it was guilt

But doubt that's how I truly felt.

And why not *coitus interruptus*?

Like learning how to masturbate

All that is I developed late;

I feared that I would be inept as

Lover of such a giantess,

Fourteen emotionally and crass.

29

Oxford was kind to me, a peasant.

My last night-journey home; daybreak

Would bring my dad, faithfully present,

Waiting for me, a firm handshake,

And then to other much-loved faces.

I'd bought, at Oxford station, *Isis*,

The student mag, and was surprised

To find a piece I recognised,

A sub-Lawrentian short story

About a young man craving sin

I had forgotten I'd sent in.

It didn't give me dreams of glory,

But *you can write* it seemed to hint,

This first thing of my own in print.

30

Better as scholar than as lover,

But fearful—I had not rehearsed

My Vivas... Turning the card over

I said in awe, 'I've got a First.'

Immediately my father ordered,

'Get in the car!' That I'd afforded

Him pride, to part-repay the love

He'd given, I valued far above

My own pride. So we went careening

All over; he'd burst in, half-crazed,

'Donald's got a First!' Then I was praised,

Though few of them could grasp its meaning.

My stingiest uncle, Leslie's, joy

Made him rash: 'Five bob for 'ee, boy!'

31

Dad's car, new-old, much weather-beaten,

Was the first one he could afford

Since the T-Ford he'd shipped to Britain

From Hollywood, when like a lord

In Carnkie he had cut a figure,

A stylish young man in full vigour.

Now, in his fifties, lined and worn,

He seemed defeated and forlorn.

Mum boosted him, just as the car did,

And it was mum who reckoned that

He'd look good in a trilby hat,

His workingman's flat cap discarded.

Stylish herself, she liked him dressed

With dignity in his Sunday best.

32

Facing me was a harder trial

Than Oxford Finals: wedding day.

As the day neared I felt denial,

Wished it were many moons away.

'Telegram of congratulations

From George the Sixth!' Shock, acclamation.

My cousin Gerald, with a sly

Smile: 'Oh no, it's George and Vi!'

I'd spent the service, with great choices

Of hymns, as if I floated far

Above, heard my dad plunge, mum soar.

That sole recording of their voices,

An LP, was years later smashed

By Maureen when her tolerance crashed.

33

Our honeymoon choice, because I valued

The Romantics, was our northern Lakes;

After the first parts of *The Prelude*

I know it's hard to stay awake,

But some of the Lucy verse is radiant.

Our train chugged slowly up a gradient,

After two long rides and a night

In London, mountains at last in sight.

Glancing out, I saw two chaps putting

Just yards away on a golf green.

I stared, then jerked; I touched Maureen

Who looked up, laid aside her knitting.

'The shorter one, who's lining up

His club to putt... I know that chap!'

34

I took her to my army training,

To our Lance-Jack from Lancashire

In his broad northern brogue disdaining

The efforts of an officer

To have lads sign for longer service

For extra pay. This Lance-Jack: *'Jarvis,*

Noo one from Wigan ever saigns on.'

Now I was watching his ball run

And miss the hole by inches. Plumper

Than he had been five years ago,

His cheeks now with a ruddier glow,

Not khaki but bright mustard jumper.

We moved on and he disappeared.

'To see him here today—how weird!'

35

So here I was, it all seemed dreamlike,

In marriage and in Windermere;

And peaks that vanished made life seem like

Chimera that would disappear.

Like, blandly, Mrs Morley's dishes,

Although her coffee was delicious.

And often, on a crumbling track,

I'd think about my old Lance-Jack;

His sudden appearance was surreal,

Much more than a coincidence;

He'd spoken with such blunt good sense

Jarvis's crazy thought to foil,

Signing on for an extra year...

A lifetime I had signed up for.

36

She smartly frocked, I not yet scruffy,

My college blazer every night.

But after after-dinner coffee

I'd take a walk, in fading light.

As we'd be fine all day together

Out sightseeing, I'd wonder whether

She sensed I felt hysterical

From claustrophobia, and how well,

After five years, she really knew me.

Or I myself... I gulped the air,

Sought girls late-walking the lake shore,

A helpless yearning running through me

At a girl's voice, in darkness, faint.

Love, sex. Till death. I can't. I can't.

Four

Death and enchantment

1

I started teaching at a Grammar

School on the mild south Devon coast,

Coed, and in my psychodrama

A valuable staging-post.

Two Grammars, boys and girls, had plighted

Their troth, but not yet quite united:

I'd speak more curtly to, say, 'Smith',

More gently when addressing 'Beth'.

It was to be, by choice, my crash course

In learning not to be so shy

With females; I know some would say,

By our harsh rules, it was a rash course,

Young hormones meaning danger lurked;

But as a shyness cure it worked.

2

In my first year there the world ended

I felt, because my father died

As January snow descended.

That night it was easy to decide

That mum, Maureen and I would tumble

Into their bed. I heard mum fumble

Her corset off in the dark, the slight

Jingle it makes. That darkest night

We giggled at it. And in the morning,

Mum gone, I fiercely fucked my wife

To bring my father back to life

The only way I knew of scorning

Death. His much loved *News Chronicle*

Arrived. Why was it published still?

3

The bus I caught, attending numbly

To death's affairs, held only two

Women, their backs to me, rustic, homely,

From one of the hamlets the bus passed through

Rounding Carn Brea, dour and mine-pitted.

One of the women, as she knitted:

'I 'eard 'Arold Thomas, up Carnkie, died.'

'Sure 'nuff?' I knew the woman lied,

All else had died, not dad. I hated

The old soul who in the very next breath

Spoke of whist drives, Recording the death

In Camborne my anger was not sated,

I would have killed her had I a knife.

The funeral passed, I went on with life.

4

My teaching helped me: the comradely

Humour, like in my sixth form class

A dreamy girl but sitting staidly

Suddenly fell back on her ass

While I was mentioning the dilemma,

Perhaps part sexual, of Emma.

Or when all quoted, on advice,

'We pissed along the polished ice'

Instead of 'hissed' in mock exams and

They knew I'd laugh. The culprit, plain,

I often walked with from the train;

Lin was as Devonshire as damson.

We met years later; I was stunned,

So gorgeous... became a lifelong friend.

5

It felt both healing and heartbreaking

To bring into that drawing room

A year on, with the loss still aching,

The first fruits of my young wife's womb,

Caitlin. All four were hunched together

Silent, my uncle, aunts and mother

In half-dark, a small fire in the grate.

We brought a tiny Christmas light.

This was the room whose green Venetian

Blinds called to mind when mummy brought

Me there to my granny, her skin taut

Over her bones, a frightening vision,

I seventeen months, she soon to die;

She gave me green grapes, blessing me.

6

At school, the mood was easy going,

Long before sexual politics;

I recall plump Miss Gale (French) showing,

As though she posed for *Span* or *Spick*

(Which I'd still slily buy) a hearty

Thigh at a seniors' Christmas party.

A game was ending in which rough

Boys 'helped' the girls take nylons off;

She was re-clipping a suspender

And warmly smiled, catching my gaze.

Those were less puritanic days,

More masters' eyes than mine would wander

To stair-climbs of the sixth form streams,

Their Jacob's ladder stocking seams.

7

Forgive me, for I know it's boring,

This harping on a fetish note,

For me, though, it is reassuring,

A comfort, for the stern Lord smote

'St. Martin's Villa'. Auntie Cecie,

From her loved Harold's death half-crazy,

Died, and the house could not survive.

I strove to keep it half-alive,

In vain. The others had to scatter,

Nellie into a loveless Home,

Eddie to in-laws; only mum

Stayed, as a tenant. But there was greater

Damage, Carnkie, without our clan,

Lost too much, its slow death began.

8

Maureen and I lived in a rented

Flat, and our home life smoothly ran.

No postwar working-class wife resented

Housework—everything spick and span,

To use an idiom I was versed in.

Speaking of verse, I was immersed in

Writing and sending poems out.

My main urge was to write about

What in my life was sadly lacking:

Women, sex, passion. There was I,

With soon a second child, a boy,

And all my hot blood knew of fucking

Was with my wife. How could I write

From an experience so slight?

9

After four years we moved from Devon.

My lectureship, in Hereford,

Was all I'd ever ask of heaven.

We found at last we could afford

To buy a small house and a second-

Hand car. My new post appeared fecund

Potentially, and so it proved.

I'd teach the authors I most loved

To girls from eighteen upwards, sprawled in

Comfy armchairs, and allowed to smoke.

I chose the texts that would provoke

Deep thought and also would embolden

These girls to open wide the gates

Of feeling; so, Donne, Lawrence, Yeats...

10

I met, for coffee, on a London

Trip my old Devonshire pupil, Lin,

So changed, so ardent, that with abandon

We fucked till the dawn came creeping in.

In Edinburgh, we heard the Mahler

Eighth, and left our bed in squalor,

Such that the guest house lady said,

'You two are awfu' fond of yer bed.'

But then, in London, she found another,

And it was time. We resumed the affair

When she'd become a pensioner

But decorously, having to smother

Arthritic pain and smoker's cough

To come—then hysterically laugh.

11

'You've lovely legs!' I called out, smiling.

Long, shapely legs were coming down

Broad stairs, and they were so beguiling!

The girl smiled as Maureen had done.

I had no thought of my dad's greeting

To my first wife at their first meeting,

It had to have been some higher voice

Decreeing both must be my choice.

I asked her could we meet soon after.

She narrowed grey-green eyes and spat,

'You're married! That's disgraceful!' That

Seemed that. A Christmas party: laughter

Between us as balloons we poked,

Leaping high. Her resistance broke.

12

We drove in my old Vauxhall Viva

To rough ground on a moonlit night,

And when we kissed I knew I'd never

Known kisses where my soul took flight,

Not kisses, more one kiss unbroken

Except to breathe. I made a token

Advance in sliding her skirt back

Beyond her front suspenders, black;

She moved my hand away, but gently,

Saying, 'You want too much too soon,'

In her soft, semi-Cockney croon.

Her 'too soon' thrilled me; evidently

I pleased her too: wrote, decades on,

'He showed he was a gentleman.'

13

If only, as I do with Russia's

Great poets—not too badly—I

Knew to translate Denise's luscious

Kisses to words! Can't even try.

But I recall, if I was glancing

Askance, that I would find entrancing

The way her upper lip would rise,

Reveal a glint of white, her eyes

Closed. I thought she resembled Leda

In art—but ravishing the Swan.

I swear a single current ran,

But spreading out like an armada,

Between her soft lips and her cunt,

A word she liked, her nature blunt.

14

Though in her young days she was slender

She had substantial hips and thighs,

A perfect frame for her suspender

Belts, always black; it won't surprise

That this became a major focus;

Jacob's *terribile est locus*,

'How awesome is this place' could be

My own reaction. Carelessly

She'd cross her long legs, well aware of

The effect on me and other men

Glimpsing her nylon's broad welt strain.

There's never been, I swear, a pair of

Legs so alluring, and Denise

Knew how to flash, to thrill and tease.

15

Till almost thirty, just one woman,

And mostly spent in all-male spheres.

Once Lin had ended my long famine

I'd hoped to make up for lost years.

Maureen and our small children happy,

I'd seen no reason not to copy

The Byronic Don; but when I found

Denise, the urge to play around

Went, and I knew I must abandon

The excuse of after-hours events

At college, and all such pretence;

No parapet of lies to stand on,

As it's impossible to keep

Secret a passion that goes deep.

16

Somehow I had to find the courage.

I asked my wife to sit with me.

'Maureen, I'd like an open marriage.'

I was having an affair, but she

Would always be, I said, my centre.

And there was nothing to prevent her

From dating men outside as well.

She turned pale, trembled, the tears fell.

Leave me? But I was the breadwinner,

We'd two small children, Caitlin, Sean,

So much to lose these eight years on

From when I took those after-dinner

Pacings beside Lake Windermere,

Tormented, gulping the free air.

17

Beloved legs up Yeats's Tower,

The winding stair... a pilgrimage

And lovefest. Bleeding Hearts would lour

At us, and B&B landlords rage,

Hearing the English guests, unmarried,

Fucking—through thin walls the sound carried.

We found the tumulus of Queen Maeve

On Knocknarea, and Yeats's grave,

Then, after lost and jolted riding,

A derelict house my mind knew well

In the light of evening, 'Lissadell'.

Last, in a pub, carefully hiding

Our feelings, watched as England won

The football World Cup. Then it was done.

18

Licensed to teach, Denise was heading

South-east, to take a primary post,

Near her home village Ash, in Reading.

The previous intimacy was lost,

But we stood firm: we must maintain our

Affair, meet often, either by train or

By car. But after a few weeks,

All colour draining from my cheeks,

I received from her a 'Dear John' letter:

She loved me, but... was seeing her

Old boyfriend, a Surrey cricketer,

Her age. He offered her a better

Future than could a married man...

My tears made her handwriting run.

19

I rang, and begged her for a meeting.

Just for ten minutes, she replied.

I drove two hundred miles; her greeting

Was just as cold. I know I cried

Most of the way back; I had lost her,

And couldn't bear it. From Ash to Gloucester,

Unable to accept the truth,

I stopped at every red phone booth

To ring her home. She wasn't present—

Was out with *him*—but there was some

Bleak comfort that this was her home.

When I reached mine, Maureen was pleasant,

Compassionate, tried to console—

I believe genuinely, on the whole.

20

I spent a term, as Visiting Poet,

At Hamlyn University, chaste,

Strict Methodist (and one soon knew it)

In Minnesota's wintry waste.

I learned to chainsmoke there, relieving

Thereby my loneliness and grieving,

And cigs, in the U.S., were cheap.

More cheering would have been to sleep

With students, but I found that many

Were being counselled by the Dean.

I slept with one, who spilled the beans

Straight from my bed. It seemed uncanny,

Being chastised by the President

When I still bore her musky scent.

21

Each week the surly Bursar urged me

To have a student clean my flat.

'I'm fine, thanks.' For they would have charged me.

Cleaning? I saw no need for that,

For three months' dust is not unpleasant,

Unlike the tumbling snow, incessant.

In truth, I badly missed Maureen,

Our cosy fires, homely cuisine,

The local diner quickly souring.

When spring came in a furnace-burst

I daily played Delius's *First*

Cuckoo in Spring, and yearned for flowering

May trees, and luscious English glades,

Their blend of sunlit grass and shades.

22

A bank clerk stopped her Studebaker

One midnight, spread her thighs, lay back:

'Okay, you want it'—let me take her

Between long garters (U.S.), black.

It's quite a wistful recollection

Because I found some weird infection

As I flew home had swathed in tights

All women, banishing the delights

Associated with suspenders!

Beneath the skirt one vast expanse

Of nylon, nothing straining, tense,

None of the drama. All one gender!

A revolution quite as bad

As Lenin's coup in Petrograd.

23

—At least for me and many other

Men—a majority—and I

Hated that women didn't bother

To think of the complexity

Of male desire, male symbolism;

And we, from fear or masochism,

Sat dumb as magic feminine

Attire went to the rubbish bin.

There might have been some consultation!

What was a normal taste before

For something every woman wore

Would seem a weird, odd aberration.

My sister's bluey increased grief:

'I'm wearing pantsuits, with relief.'

24

I felt one day a sudden yearning

To reach Denise. And fortune smiled:

I heard her voice, my stomach churning.

She told me she had been with child;

Ian had broken their engagement;

We'd met once during our estrangement,

He'd found my mail in her handbag,

Thought the child mine, and she a slag.

She'd had a son; it was adopted,

She was at home recovering.

So she was free! I wished to sing!

Asked could we meet, and she accepted.

'Come to a party, Friday night,'

I urged, and she replied, 'Alright.'

25

I met her train at Worcester station.

It seemed we'd never been apart.

I've never felt such pure elation

As then, such singing in my heart.

We were at one again together,

It was a day of sunny weather,

Green, luscious England spread out wide.

She raised her green skirt at the side,

Re-clipping a suspender. Glory!

'Still stockings, then?' 'Oh yes; I hate

Tights, they're so clinging.' Thus the Fates

Spoke through her in those ordinary

Half-Cockney tones a miracle!

She must have known that it would thrill.

26

After that visit we decided

She'd be our house-guest each weekend,

Our wondering children would be guided

To see Denise as a 'good friend'.

It wasn't as hard as one imagines,

She had a way with kids, as legions

Would testify, and gave ours love.

A family meal, and then we'd move

Discreetly to... what was essential.

As the months went by, rumours spread

And gossip—who with whom in bed.

Sean, with his writerly potential,

Would say, when schoolmates tried to scar,

'My dad's descended from a Tsar'—

27

His way of facing down the stigma.

At weekends we had much the same

Arithmetical enigma

As I've observed of my first home:

Five sometimes, only four bed spaces.

At eighty five one's memory hazes;

Sean's bedroom was the smallest one;

Denise slept there, so where did Sean

Sleep? I don't know! I would caress her,

We'd fuck, in that tight single bed;

After an hour I'd lay my head

Beside Maureen's, lightly embrace her

Flannelette-nightied, turned-aside form

Already asleep, cosily warm.

28

A scene more comic than erotic:

We'd sometimes drink with Maureen and

Her latest 'friend'. I'm paralytic,

Find at midnight I cannot stand.

Both girls between them push and pull me

Upstairs, I groaning, then they hurl me

Onto the righteous double bed.

I feel each tugging as I shed

My trousers. The usual drunk poet.

I lie in shirttails and y-fronts,

Such a ridiculous circumstance.

Denise's voice: 'I'll leave you to it!'

Chuckles uneasily and goes.

Such an ironic light that throws.

29

Each girl was jealous of the other,

Denise of Maureen in her role

Of the established wife and mother,

Maureen of who possessed my soul.

Once Denise came back after shopping,

Lit up her Rothman's before dropping

The casual phrase, 'I couldn't find

A red suspender belt'—unkind

Perhaps to Maureen, who grew snappy.

In time, as months and then years passed,

The freshness of it all was lost,

The sex staled, meetings were less happy.

Eagerly I was waiting for

A short American reading tour.

30

At our first stop I slept with Carol,

A teacher, pleasant, slightly bland;

I toured with Redgrove, who was moral

Surprisingly—lovesick—I found.

'Don fucked, I drank,' he'd laugh. In Tucson

I fell for a striking tall girl, Susan,

Her long straight wheaten hair, her eyes

Warm blue as the Sonoran skies.

The sex—not great, but I would settle

For beauty. It amused Peter, chaste

All three weeks; his heart only raced

Phoning his new love, Penny Shuttle.

Through much of the long homeward flight

I'd Susan's photo in my sight.

31

I took the train home, jetlagged, knowing

Denise would visit in two days;

With Susan's shimmering hair still glowing

The journey was a dreamy haze;

She was both gone, impossibly distant,

Yet here, so beautiful, insistent

And all-consuming, no mirage,

Yet soon, God help me, our *ménage*

A trois... Denise arrived, we gathered

For supper, and then filled with dread

In Sean's room, perching on the bed

Awkwardly, shamefaced, hot and bothered,

I unwrapped what I'd bought for her,

An *ersatz* Aztec calendar.

32

She liked it. And now what? Deceive her?

It would be easiest, but I found

Again I could not but uncover

Emotions that were so profound,

Or so I thought. Hence—a confession.

She didn't lose her self-possession

But listened understandingly.

'Have you a photo?... Can I see?'

Careful, not wanting to make creases,

I handed it to her. She smiled,

Astounding me, her mood so mild;

Then ripped it into little pieces.

So all that sympathy was staged!

'That's unforgivable!' I raged.

33

She gave me no time to recover;

A year ago, on the school trip—

Did I recall it?—a camp at Dover,

After the children were asleep

She and her fellow teacher, Barry,

Had stolen out for a pub curry.

Young, married—she thought unhappily—

A really nice chap, painfully shy.

Returned, it was ages before he kissed her,

And his hand trembled as he rucked

Her skirt up. And, well, they had fucked.

'And had he known you wear...' I asked her,

My words half-choking in my throat.

'Yes—when I stretched up for my coat.'

34

I was now trembling, my heart racing

With jealous excitement, a weird blend.

I think by now we were undressing.

'I can recall he ran his hand

Under my stocking, like this'—showing

Me how he did it, before going

On with her story. The next night

During their fuck it didn't feel right—

Till she recalled she had a tampon

In her! A few times this past year

They'd fucked; but this month's camp—no more,

His enraged wife had put a clamp on

His fling—a grin on Denise's face—

She had found condoms in his case.

35

We were in bed now, wildly fucking,

She in suspender belt and hose,

Her lips and cunt engorged, insucking,

And now and then I'd interpose

A question, my voice thick and throaty.

Forgotten, that resplendent beauty,

The swiftly fading desert plant.

'What did you say when he said I want'...

Some lurid mid-sex phrase—'Well, do so!'

We went on fucking through the night,

We fucked to set our ghosts aflight,

My passion for her blazed anew, so

Wondrous that journey was; till we

Collapsed. Then, 'Don, make us a cup o' tea.'

36

I made the tea; we could have drunk all

The nearby Wye; slept for a while;

Then Maureen's shout up: 'Don, a phonecall,

Someone for you!' Oh bloody hell!

Pulled on my robe and, wobbly, shaken,

Went down. 'Hello?' A softly spoken

'Don, hi! It's Carol.' American

Accent. Who's Carol? My head spun,

And then I knew: pre-Arizona,

That girl... 'I had some holiday,

Had never been to the UK;

I'm at the Dragon, round the corner.

Can we meet up?' So long a trek

By air and train, in wild hope. Fuck!

37

She sounded plaintive, nervous, humble;

What idiocy it was to splurge

A fortune on a crazy gamble;

And yet I understood the urge,

Thinking our brief liaison fateful,

To go for broke, not be regretful.

'I'm very busy, can't spare more

Than an hour—a coffee.' A downcast, 'Sure.'

I tried to do what she expected—

Lay down with her, and did my best

From sympathy to pretend lust,

But that-which-can't-be-fooled objected.

I pleaded jetlag, staggering off,

But in truth fucked out, and in love.

Five

Juggling

1

She must move near; this had been scary

For both. In flat, featureless countryside

A house we found, redbrick, quite dreary,

Around it even birdsong died;

A house, you would surmise, for loners,

Victorian; the married owners

Were mixed race, with one teenage lad,

Black. Within weeks my mistress had

An attic flat there: perfect setting,

One felt, for the mad wife in *Jane Eyre*;

Sombre, the last steep, narrow stair.

She settled in, and worked at getting

A teaching post, and one soon came,

For she was brilliant, a Head's dream.

2

It was a relief, now, to be able

To see her most days of the week,

Making the relationship more stable,

Providing too a welcome break

For Maureen, now allowed some head room,

Denise elsewhere, Sean in his bedroom

Not she and I. On Saturdays

I would sleep over with Denise

After a steak at the 'Imperial',

With barley wine, a favourite then.

The week nights, when I left by ten,

Were mostly placid, not venereal,

But always I would run my hand

To where our talisman would be found.

3

Then an adventure and confession

As it was happening, and I

Loved it, as it involved obsession.

The owners' sixteen year old boy

Would intercept Denise returning

From school, to chat. It was a burning

June, and when she had reached her flat

She would strip off her blouse and skirt

And lie in her cool bedroom, covered

By a sheet. One afternoon—a shock:

She heard a key grate in the lock.

She thought it the boy, for she'd discovered

A rumpled drawer. Presumably

He was entering with his mother's key.

4

That knowledge calmed, for she had only

To scream, his mum would run up fast.

She'd found him decent, shy and lonely,

A black lad shunned—and sex-obsessed

Of course. She lay with her eyes closed and

Hoped he would leave—but then was frozen

Feeling the thin sheet on her rise

And a soft touch on her bare thighs

Above the stockings, heard his breathing,

Excited. Then just as silently

He'd gone. All this she shared with me

That evening. I felt envy seething,

I was in Melbourne once again;

This boy had touched as well as seen!

5

We were both outraged and admiring.

It was unconscionable, yet...

He'd shown extraordinary daring!

Her eyes flared like her cigarette.

I loved her psyche, anarchic, spirited,

From gypsy ancestors inherited,

Always refusing to conform,

As in her veering from the norm

Of tights and trousers. We discussed it;

He meant no ill, so she should not

Act any differently, we thought,

See what he'd do next. The lad lusted

For her, no shrivilled-up schoolma'am,

And that was natural: what harm?

6

Next day, she told me, the boy came and

His touch had turned to a soft stroke.

On the third day her anarchic daimon

Whispered she should still more provoke.

There is a hint, in the oppressive

Heat, with her lonely, him obsessive,

Of princess in the tower. But then,

'The bugger had a finger in!'

Sounds unlike myth. Unless she dreamt it

Or fantasised I'm sure in age

His life's book opens to that page

Where he touched heaven. I attempted

To make her still more thrill and shock,

But sensibly she changed the lock.

7

In dying Carnkie, where my mother

Lived, I was Donald, happy with

Maureen, because they knew no other.

In Cornwall, usually West Penwith,

Distant enough on a vacation

To avoid encountering friend or relation,

I'd drive to Carnkie, furtively

Pick my mum up. By this time she

Was badly crippled by arthritis.

I'd drive us to a discreet motel

To join Denise. They got on well.

Despite her pain, mum's smile was bright as

Ever. We would have lunch, then

Guiltily I'd drive her home again.

8

Visiting five nights out of seven

As time went on grew onerous,

I'd feel relieved if I was given

An excuse to stay in my own house.

As for Denise, who could be fiery

Enough to wreck the calmest priory,

She'd storm, could see no fruitful end,

She could not even meet my friends.

Outside of school and me, the only

People she met were at my home,

For sometimes, I at work, she'd come

To see my children. She was lonely,

Childless, still grieving for her son;

Saturday sex became routine.

9

I almost welcomed when the river,

Flooding, sidled towards our house;

There'd be a not unpleasant shiver

As sandbags were dropped off for us;

We'd take it as a family game as

We moved upstairs with food and primus;

Our old piano raised on bricks,

If Wye seeped in—it's not the Styx!

At night, no poet, lover, dreamer,

Just watchful father, I'd wake up

And go to see the waters lap

Around us, under streetlights shimmer,

Pleased I could not go anywhere

Till the Wye ebbed. But floods were rare.

10

Thinking of that, I recall a morning

When mum, at Greyfriars, saw pass by

A sight that seemed comic—with no warning

Youths in shorts heading for the Wye,

Bearing on their shoulders towards the river

A long boat. It seems to last forever,

And mum bursts out, 'See they g'eat 'ores!'

Then, tickled by what she's said, she roars.

We all laughed too—so unexpected

She could think of whores! Each year she spent

Two weeks with us, when I still went

Elsewhere most evenings. She elected

To keep mum, not reveal she knew

Denise; so her life was split too.

11

How could I find an extra night off,

Relieve Denise's loneliness

And boredom, and by some sleight of

Hand, harmlessly for us both, increase

Mutual desire? She craved more knowledge,

Might like to learn French. At the college

The head of French was a bachelor,

Middle-aged, with an old-maidish air,

Soft, safe. I asked him would he tutor

A friend of mine, if he could spare

An evening. Up the last, steepling stair

One night, to see if he would suit her,

I followed both; two pairs of eyes

Gazed up at welts, gleams of white thighs.

12

It seemed to work well; he was pleasant,

She said, although a mother's boy,

Bashful with women. I was present

For drinks one night, saw her employ

Her skirt-hem trickery, amusing

Us both by obviously confusing

The poor chap: why did Don not mind

Her on her knees, crawling around

The carpet, showing her suspenders?

More weeks passed. He was impotent

He had confessed to her. We went

To Greece, and gloried in its splendours,

Its sacred groves and oracles,

Funded by softporn articles.

13

I bought a statuette in Delphi

Of Leda and the Swan. Returned,

I crazily, bats in the belfry,

Wanting to see if I discerned—

It was their evening of tuition—

Anything sexual, on a mission

To find what I wanted yet did not want,

A hypocrite and a lying cunt,

I rushed upstairs, saw Denise scurry

Into the bathroom, too quick to see

If she was dressed, then dervishly

Geoff whirling round. She or a Fury

Returned. I saw her eyes were red.

'Geoff was just comforting me,' she said.

14

Next time I saw her, sitting rigid

She said her tears were from despair;

She'd called at Greyfriars; Maureen, frigid,

Had banned her from coming any more.

It made her see our situation

Was hopeless. Then came devastation:

We had to part; Geoff offered her

Friendship, a time to clear the air.

A stone face greeted all my pleading:

At most we could meet once a week,

She'd let me take her for a steak.

Blinded by tears my heart was bleeding

I drove home from that thunderbolt,

Knowing that it was all my fault.

15

That hot, dire summer I found a haven

Deep in the lush, green countryside

With Andrew, dour, white-suited, unshaven,

One student lover or other beside

Him in the garden, endless wine flowing;

Then when the endless sun was going,

But promising another fine

Morning, into the cool house, Caroline,

His wife, abed. Then endless Bruckner,

For Andrew, colleague and best friend,

Would never want the day to end,

For neither wine nor girl he'd fuck nor

Sleeping pills saved him; when he slept

No dog but a snarling black wolf leapt.

16

So I endured, griefstricken, zestless;

Met her for steak, and once we lay

And fucked, but she seemed spectral, listless,

And scarcely moved. Then came a day

She sent for me. Without emotion

She said she'd just had an abortion.

Her face was white, she lay in bed.

'But he was impotent, you said.'

Such challenges she'd always rise to,

I should know that!—with a wan smile.

'When I told Geoff, he ran a mile,

But sent nice flowers. And then flies to

His mum. He wasn't right for me.'

I hugged her, poured out love and tea.

17

Later, relieved, I was also frightened:

She'd been almost lost to me; and though

My fright I typically lightened

With tipsy banter, asked her how

She had seduced him into losing

His impotence, found it amusing

Now I was sure that he was gone,

I knew that something must be done

To keep her: a baby. There was no other

Way. But she taught in a church school,

And in those days the iron rule

Was to dismiss a single mother.

So, marriage; it was the only course.

But first, less pleasant still—divorce.

18

I gave a feeble explanation

For why I needed a divorce,

Some nonsense about liberation,

'But nothing here will change, of course,

I simply want to breathe more freely.

No need to tell the kids; it's really

A technicality, no more.'

And soon I lied in court—I swore

We shared a house but nothing further;

Kept out of print the quick decree.

Maureen reacted sorrowfully,

Nor could I have expected other.

I was a juggler, desperate

To hold life in a steady state.

19

It was a time of shock and grieving,

Deepest of all, the death of mum.

Beside me when I was receiving

The call, Denise wished she could come

To the funeral, for they liked each other;

But husband, wife, must go together.

I too would have preferred to have

Denise with me at the open grave.

A few years later, while returning

From a Cornish holiday, she said

Mum shone down, from a sky of lead,

Saying, 'Look after him'... A mourning

Postponed, dwarfed by her death, the news

The college I loved was marked to close.

20

What do the atheists say that's better,

I wondered, seeing her smile in death,

Out of pain now and younger, lighter,

Than her deep, simple Christian faith?

Nothing, I thought, sweet hymns sustaining

Me as the few old souls remaining

In Carnkie who knew her did their best

To sing her to a quiet rest

Where she would see once more her handsome

Harold. All she had left was in three

Paper bags: she had given away

All but her soul, worth a king's ransom.

Her card for my fortieth was at home

Awaiting me, signed 'Lovingly, mum'

21

And now, a secret wedding. Tipsy

By elevenses, plied with brandies by

Her dad, swart, black-haired, of gypsy

Descent; Denise, green-suited, her eye

On him, a danger in his crazy

Periods; voices, Cockney, racy,

Of uncles, aunts; I suffering in

Best suit and tie; her mum, sour, thin

And silent, thoroughly disapproving

Our marriage, although hardly more so

Than I, in her parents' bungalow.

'It's almost time, we should be moving.'

'Time for one more', says George, her dad.

Why am I here? Like George, I'm mad.

22

We trooped off to the registry office,

I drunk and shaky at the knees,

Lied all the time through the bland service

Although I deeply loved Denise.

A put-u-up was our thalamal

Bed; it was like sleeping on a camel,

Still I was eager for a fuck.

She feared her dad would go berserk—

Twice she had threatened him with a poker

When, crazed, he was moving in to glass

Her mum, and she was his 'princess',

The wall thin. She did let me take her,

But gently, we scarcely moved at all,

And she kept looking at the wall.

23

I dropped her off at her apartment,

Relieved the travesty was behind,

Now silence in which to write; but that meant

First greeting Maureen and her kind,

Fat, rich, married car salesman lover.

We need a different term to cover

Someone our children and my ex-wife

Needed to have some kind of life.

'How was your weekend?' 'Oh, quite pleasant,

A good performance of *Rosmersholm*,

And then we saw Jane Austen's home.

But God, the rain! It was incessent.'

Something like that. I must have felt

Awful, but I blanked out the guilt.

24

Caitlin says now I was always there for

Her, although I was often gone,

Felt certain of my love and care, for

Her problems I would ponder on,

Offer wise words a few days after.

And she recalls the hoots of laughter

At Sunday dinners I'd provoke

With what they called 'dad's Sunday joke'.

Sean shrieked once that I was the weakest

Man living; but when Leeds lost the Cup

I grieved for him; and felt banged up

Like him when he was at his bleakest

On a false rape charge. I did mind

Immensely, but day by day was blind.

25

Often my thoughts would be diverted

To churning mental images,

For it was in these years I started

A novel, to cheer depressive days,

Since teaching in a dying college

Is sad, just like a dying village.

I'd never thought I'd write in prose

And all my inexperience shows

In *Birthstone*; but I found great pleasure

In literally *making* new

Friends as my cast of people grew.

However, poems leave some leisure

Between them; novels once begun

Take your mind over till they're done.

26

Denise was, as she had twice proved, fecund,

Her womb, soul, longing to be filled;

In a few months the love-child quickened;

I was content that she was thrilled,

Although I felt an underlying

Unease, my piled-up secrets weighing

On me. As the months passed, I'd blank

My fears, more copiously drank.

School governors, seeing her belly spreading,

Summoned her kindly Head to insist

Single Miss Aldred be dismissed.

'Ah, but she's married!' Showed her wedding

Certificate with a sly grin,

Leaving them mortified, in a spin.

27

She had made friends at last, both teachers,

Welsh, chapel-going, but liked a dram,

Lived their faith truly, without being preachers

Of it to us. We felt at home

With them, round their piano singing.

Rock music on, we were soon bringing

Our bawdier natures, and Denise

Performed a partial, slow striptease

At my cajoling. Stunned, they said it

Was elegant, and Cath was moved

To shop for clothes, a move approved

By Roger; so I take the credit

For re-converting her from tights.

It vastly refreshed, they said, their nights.

28

We felt an easiness in their presence;

They brought back 'Beverly' to me,

For they were working-class in essence,

Generous with hospitality,

Down-to-earth, humble and kind-hearted.

Like me they'd never far departed

From the Celtic roots from which they'd sprung,

Mining and chapel, rugby, song.

Denise had an open invitation

To visit, I elsewhere engaged,

And I was pleased, for it assuaged

Her sense of being in isolation.

They'd two small daughters, who would come

To see her as a second mum.

29

Another divorce, more real and painful:

My college by government order closed.

For fifteen years, always disdainful

Of pedagogy, we'd exposed

Our students to the masterpieces

Of literature, from ancient Greece's

To Eliot, Joyce, Saul Bellow, Frost;

Seminars over, the talk crossed

With the same zest into the kitchen:

Was Anna Karenina right to leave

Her son? then gradually inweave

With what our coffee breaks were rich in—

Laughter, students and staff at one,

Anecdotes, gossip, wittiness, fun.

30

Around the kitchen's strewn used crockery.

All's silent now as Yorick's grave,

No more the talk, the jokes, the mockery,

Bright faces; all had left now save

For a staid girl and I, united

By sadness, mute, as if sedated.

On impulse: 'Would you like a ride?'

'Alright.' Through lush June countryside

We rode, mute still, I hardly knew her.

But when we reached the Malvern Hills

Alive with Elgar's music still,

Not I but summer's sadness drew her

Down, beneath sun and clouds like wool,

To fuck, and it was beautiful.

31

Denise in pregnancy was often

Angry—angry I didn't quit

Maureen. Our new friends tried to soften

Her rage, but when Denise would sit

At table, banging her whisky tumbler,

Arousing their little girls from slumber

With shouts for hours and wouldn't stop

When all the rest were fit to drop,

Her normal kindness turned demonic.

In all ways generous to a fault

She shot more barbs with every malt,

Their homely lounge become Byronic.

I often, drunk, grinding the gears,

Drove home at 5 a.m., in tears.

32

Today, through half a century's distance,

I appreciate the sacrifice

She made, her loyalty, persistence:

A week's hard teaching, then the race

To come to me, but always sharing

For years—how infinitely wearing

And loving. And then recklessly

Quitting home, job, to live near me.

And now to be a single mother,

Having to juggle work and child...

It is no wonder she felt riled,

Wished to disturb my altogether

Too comfortable life, a cook

To serve me as I wrote a book.

33

All I could feel then was to fear her

Dark moods—in one, she bit my hand,

And as the time of birth came nearer

Began to feel I couldn't stand

Being a dad again, and harried

At home—they didn't know I'd married.

And now to say I had a son

Or daughter... And there was someone

I'd met—that's often in the picture—

Blonde, lovely, on a writing course;

Liz, from Snowdonia, wrote verse

And painted, was gentle, wouldn't hector.

I'd given Denise a child at least.

I'd break away! And did. Released!

34

It was midwinter, the roads icy,

An accident and I would freeze,

But Liz's curry, fragrant, spicy,

Soon warmed me up. I heard Denise

Had given birth to a son. The slightest

Tremor went through me. But the brightest

Stars in all Britain shone above

My love nest as we made warm love.

I met a friend who'd seen Denise, an

Irish lady; said she was fine,

Had sighed, 'At least I'll have his son.'

That moved me, for whatever reason.

But I thanked God I had been saved,

In love where only the wind raved.

Six

Journeys

1

While I was home-bound from Snowdonia,

The third or fourth time I'd been there,

Something—let's call it anhedonia—

Overcame me, and I gulped free air.

I struggled with it, thought it senseless,

But then again the truth, relentless,

She was too sweet and kind and nice.

Madness, I told myself, but Christ,

I want to see Denise! Ice sang it

Under my wheels. I need the *angst*,

I could be peaceful, but no thanks!

When I got home at last I rang; it

Took ages. 'Can I see you?' 'Yes.'

She sounded pleased. 'I'm feeding Ross.'

2

She'd moved to a small house; was standing

Outside her door. I slid, fell hard

On ice, bottle of claret landing,

Smashing, scattering red. We roared.

That wine was holy, like communion.

It was the third of such reunions,

I trust that there will be a fourth.

Denise looked radiant from childbirth.

We kissed; she showed me, almost hidden

For warmth, our son, so small, so fresh,

I wondered at him. Then her warm flesh

Against me, in our ash-scattered midden.

It shocked and stirred me when I learned

Once pregnant, she'd fucked her amorous friend.

3

I use that term as a translation

Of the French *amitié amoureuse*.

She'd drop into our conversation

His name, then some drollness to amuse

Me and not scare; he was no stranger

And I knew he posed no real danger

As he intensely loved his wife,

His three kids and his pleasant life.

But this one time she'd chosen silence

Until now; well, this time at least,

For I had thought that it had ceased.

She amused and stirred in equal balance

While smoking, drinking, till she heard

The slightest sound as our son stirred.

4

By chance Ross, from the Sacred Valley,

Peru, has emailed me today;

As often, loving, tries to rally

My spirits; he quotes Lao Tze:

Look back—depressive, onwards—frightened,

So avoid both to be enlightened,

Live in the NOW. I paraphrase

Inanely, but its wisdom stays.

Shamanic, Ross would seem far distant

From mum, who saw Christ late one night

Rap on her window, ask, 'Alright?'

But in our genes is a persistent

Faith that eternal love is near.

Mum: 'You're lookin' after me, dear.'

5

Thirty years on, in England, Lois

Came back into my still split lives;

I'd see the station platform glow as

Doors opened and, through hugs and waves,

Appeared a tiny highheeled figure,

An admiral's flagship in full rig, her

Shoes, blouse, a-glitter, her pantsuit

(Yes, alas) swaying—a recruit

To a lavish Busby Berkeley chorus.

She was fifty going on eighteen,

Jimmy or Ray? still torn between.

Too late to see the one who bore us,

And heal the 'Ray's the one, dear!' wound,

But for us both it was profound.

6

Ray dead at fifty, California

Her birthplace called; there she had veered

Between Don and Ron, with Ron the hornier,

But Don a judge. Both disappeared.

Then she to Glasgow. Our bond came—tardy

But finally strong—through Laurel and Hardy.

A spell around us they would wreathe,

We laughed till we could scarcely breathe.

She thought the cosmos was all-loving

As she was—'Call it God, or Dork...'

For California left its mark.

Eccentric—once indoors, removing

Her clothes to don her much-loved robe,

Flashing bright colours like a strobe.

7

It was hard to view her tiny figure

And see the sister who had found

By accident the way to trigger

A fetish that was so profound;

The girl whose stockinged thighs were thrilling,

Now doll-like coming downstairs trilling,

'Well, do you like my new pantsuit?'

Expecting me to find it cute—

American her intonation.

Male company she still enjoyed,

And would have flirted even with Freud.

Gone now. I miss her animation,

Her giggle, flashing perfect teeth.

Her soul's in heaven, her ash, Portreath.

8

Denise and I had agreed divorcing

When we could do it legally;

It was my method of enforcing

Between the wives equality,

To my warped thoughts. And it came easy.

In a few weeks the Decree Nisi,

Then we forgot about it. How

I told Maureen I'm not sure now.

'I have a son, and have been married

These past three years, but now I'm not.'

It was some rigmarole like that.

However, the divorce miscarried,

Some fool cocked up the Absolute.

Twenty years on we found that out.

9

Obliged to teach once she'd regained her

Strength, time with Ross that she would lose,

Needing to find a child minder,

Denise fumed at the life I chose.

I'd sworn to Maureen to be loyal,

On troubled waters she poured oil,

Whereas I feared Denise would bring

To any household *Sturm und Drang.*

I felt that there was something vengeful

In Ross-talk going on and on;

She was my Queen of Night, the moon,

Waning and waxing, ever-changeful,

Not obsessive mother. Hard to adjust

To nappy-rash displacing lust.

10

But then, her portrait in this memoir

Shows only part. I'd find Denise

Standing engrossed in Simone de Beauvoir

While at the same time grating cheese,

Tolerant of my hand remaining

For comfort upskirt, the strap straining;

Planting, or saving a hurt bird.

To isolate Eros is absurd,

The product of my own dementia.

May she forgive that sex I've stressed

As if she also was obsessed.

She hoped in her old age to venture

Into the sacred land, Tibet.

We've many lives. She'll reach there yet.

11

Reduntant, in my early forties,

I chose to write not seek a post,

Much strengthened by Maureen's support as

She said, whatever be the cost

She'd back my choice. She was an Axford

Corset—the best. But first came Oxford;

Offered a paid sabbatical,

I found myself in a small cell,

Not the grand rooms that I'd been used to.

I had signed up for a B. Litt.

I always knew that that was shit,

Believed that this time I would choose to

Live it up, drink, find sexy friends,

Then home (both homes) for long weekends.

12

Paddington station. Two girls reading,

Giggling, over a cheap dream book.

After they'd left the train at Reading

I settled back, alone. What luck!

I hadn't found the social swirl

But now the livelier, prettier girl,

Studying in Oxford, had agreed a date

On Monday, when I'd be there. Fate!

Some minutes more—a revelation:

Our meeting, talk, was in a dream

I'd had, like a coat without a seam

They were the same! Still more elation,

My psyche had foreknown, said, Look!

And she'd been reading a dream book...

13

Denise was a hurtful, helpful agent:

With our friends, having drunk a lot,

She, clearly boiling up to rage and

Distress, the air smoke-fumed and fraught,

Said that my work was mediocre.

A silence fell, and I thought, fuck her,

I'll prove it's not. And as it chanced,

While walking, smoking, deeply tranced,

One circuit of New College gardens,

I planned a novel, full of train

Journeys. I thought, all that remains

Is now to write it! Dropped the burdens

Of the Elizabethan Script

And the train-girl. Life outside stopped.

14

I wrote it on two old typewriters,

One from my youthful Oxford days;

No wives were there, the burden lighter;

Endless fag ash in two ash trays.

So it was rather schizophrenic,

With the creative joy that's manic,

Shutting all other people out.

I feel it now, in the pursuit

Of the next thought and rhyme and stanza.

The Muse's flute is distant, faint,

In these late years, but I still can't

Shut down the overwhelming sensor

That blocks even loving words as noise.

'I'm listening... I heard you...' Lies.

15

The book was done, and the obsession,

And Oxford too. I sat at home

Trying to write, stave off depression,

Hoping a new idea would come.

My college friends had mostly scattered,

And one, white-suited, who most mattered,

Andrew, had made the saddest choice.

What I was yearning for was—noise!

I missed the comradeship, the joking,

Hated the solitary life,

Once shouted at my former wife,

'This house is like a morgue, so fucking

Silent!'—'Oh, I'm so sorry, dear!'

We hugged and talked, which eased despair.

16

It's strange, my dream that was predictive,

Meeting a woman on a train

Intent on dreams, became a fictive

Train ride across a bleak terrain

Full of previsions. It was like I

Was drawing from a cosmic psyche.

But anyway, *The White Hotel*

Did quite astonishingly well;

Most pleasing, praise from genial Seamus

Heaney: it passed his jealousy test.

My tempo moved from slow to fast

As I was briefly, modestly, famous,

And on my frequent promotional tours

Had equally brief and modest amours.

17

So many sweet girls one could die for,

And I had missed out in my youth!

To Denise I had no need to lie, for

She did not wish to know the truth,

Assumed that there were fleeting creatures.

In that, we had quite different natures,

She knew I would be greatly stirred

Rather than upset when I heard,

At the right time, with whisky, brandy,

From her droll lips the latest news

Of her *amitié amoureuse*,

Like, he'd come instantly, too randy.

She knew she was my love and Muse,

Turned a blind eye to random screws.

18

When I was older but no wiser

I read a headline in the *Mail*,

'My dad's a serial womaniser',

A piece by Sean. That 'serial'

I pointed out was tautological,

Since if you womanise it's logical

It isn't something one cuts off.

'Just womaniser is enough.'

Though I believe in *hieros gamos*,

The sacred marriage, I refuse

To think, at twenty, one must choose

Till death to lie in matched pyjamas,

Two wrinkled forms, babyfaced elves,

Their whole lives wrapped up in themselves.

19

I'd say by nature I'm in tune with

The continental *cinq à sept*,

The passionate mistress, but then soon with

The caring wife, with no regret,

Sharing perhaps with laughing candour

The sauces enjoyed by goose and gander.

I felt my dad might be alive

Were his desires allowed to thrive,

His prostate working to house semen,

Deprived of which it swelled and killed;

Too much hot lust was unfulfilled.

He'd joke, about some pretty woman,

'She could put her shoes under my bed!'

Sadly I don't think any did.

20

And first and last, I'm sure, he wanted

His Amy; it is what he said

When seeming on the mend, but haunted

By new pals who'd been wheeled out dead

From the grim ward, the shadowed valley

Though hung with mistletoe, a Sally

Army band playing: 'I want to see

The green fields, Amy, and to be

With you. That's all.' But not permitted,

Alas. To him I dedicate

The girls I had from flight to flight,

City to city, as I flitted;

Each leaves with me a comely ghost,

For all were charming, warm. Well, most.

21

Erica Jong's account I cherish

Of our liaison, I her guest

At the Ritz: 'He proved entirely boorish,

Surly of manner, badly dressed.

His letters had been empathetic,

The man—snobbish, antisemitic.

I blanched when he arrived, complete

With cardboard suitcase, filled my suite

With constant smoke which made me queasy.

Thankfully he preferred to sleep

On the lounge couch so he could keep

Smoking. Only at a "greasy

Spoon" that he dragged me to was he

Relaxed: clearly an *habitué.*'

22

She labelled me 'an Irish poet',

Warned of the English libel laws.

Her piece has much that's true, although it

Perhaps exaggerates my flaws

Because her furs and leather cases

Had flown from the rich charms and graces

Of a count's palace on the Grand

Canal. I failed our one-night-stand,

Wearing a condom, but with loathing,

I can't feel in them, and stay lax;

My fear was AIDS from zipless fucks.

If I have sometimes dreamed of smoothing

My path with a partner of her class,

Moneyed, a barrister say—I pass.

23

Now this, in contrast, was romantic:

Hot day, I in some Yankee town

About to fly off translatlantic;

A woman, attractive, smart, sat down

Next to me. Delay. A conversation

Began, and effortlessly passion

Swept us away, we embraced, kissed,

The plane, the world, did not exist,

Nor airfield hazed in a heat belt.

We each of us sought to devour

The other. So, for a whole hour,

Till the command to fasten seat belts.

We straightened, read, drowsed, silent through

The long flight; shook hands at Heathrow.

24

And this—in the Gulf of Finland, singing

Loved Broadway melodies with my blonde

Guide and male editor: voices ringing,

As it seemed, to Peter and beyond,

'Where one dawn hurries to meet another'

In the white nights. Then moved, together

With other authors and my guide

Into the Finnish countryside

Of forests, lakes, at midnight tipsy

From beauty and light. But mostly I

Sat numb, as sluggish as the Wye,

Moved between Cornish mum and gypsy.

The knot was too tight to unseal;

I wrote, obsessed, so not to feel.

25

The day when normal families gather,

Christmas, I always made the least

And saddest journey; half a father

Both here and there. After the feast

Served by Maureen, the moment dreaded—

I'd rise from table and then headed

Off, leaving three mournful souls behind.

A trafficless mile away I'd find

Coolness because of my belated

Arrival, all the presents long

Opened. This way of life was wrong

For both households I knew, and hated

Myself. Somewhere I'd lost my way,

Yearned for my childhood's Christmas Day.

26

A Fellowship for a semester

States-side promised me some release,

A time of calm, but brought disaster:

Days in, I too much missed Denise.

Drunk, I typed 'thank you for your blindness'

Intending 'thank you for your kindness'.

Wildly laughing, I fell off my chair.

Gave future ill health as reason for

My midnight flit. On the Potomac

Nearby a plane had crashed; deep snow

Lay around, and they'd provided no

Phone—I'd need silence! I couldn't stomach

The loneliness, without my love,

Her acid tongue, so buggered off.

27

Brief trips were welcome; even a long one

In distance, the most memorable,

Australia, Dreamtime. I was rung, one

Morning, in my Adelaide hotel.

I'd been forewarned. 'Hi, this is Sara.'

First love... I could see shining clear her

Graceful, unearthly, freshfaced look.

'Hello!' 'My daughter's read your book.'

A poetry editor had found her.

Of course she could not remember me.

We planned to meet. I could still see

Her slim, white nape... Began to flounder

Hearing her say, 'That would be beaut!'

I'd lose that vision, so chickened out.

28

On to the city where, though fifty,

I still felt that I was fifteen:

No longer staid, conservative, thrifty,

Melbourne now wore a wealthy sheen;

Collins Street, where men dark-suited

Had crept, was lit up with x-rated

Dives, bars. I took the tram: was she

Still there, my blonde epiphany?

Well, no; but from the sprinklers spraying

Warm grass I caught the very scent

I'd smelt, and a deep yearning went

Through me. Then on; no girls were swaying,

Strap-hanging, only their white-bloused shades.

Nothing of what I felt then fades.

29

I stood outside the drab Victorian

Building where we had had our flat.

The window-tree, silent historian

Of that confused, ungainly, fat

Teenager who had lain there listening

To its rank, tropical leaves rustling,

Waiting for black legs on the sash,

Was just a wispy thin-leaved ash.

How strong was my imagination!

I saw him make his own girlfriend

From the two women close at hand,

And I felt pity and admiration.

He was still living there, although

Its present tenant would not know.

Seven

Grief and Grace

1

Ross was now eight; Denise would punish

The absent father by being cold;

Yet still, after a pleasant Cornish

Holiday we found she was with child—

At forty. I conquered my aversion

To taking life through an abortion,

Suggested it, but she was firm

And I accepted. At full term

He was born dead. She was in torment,

And I felt complicated grief.

I told Maureen, could scarce believe

That she said, 'Good!' A shocking moment,

It showed the anger she repressed—

And Caitlin and Sean had flown the nest.

2

She came back from a week in Cornwall,

I'd quite liked living in my head;

I asked her if the break had gone well

With Jack, her new friend. Yes she said.

I dived into the eggs she'd scrambled;

She, with a voice that slightly trembled:

'Would you be happier if I left?

I think you would.' I felt bereft,

Put down my fork. 'Jack wants to marry.'

I nodded. 'Yes, perhaps I would.

Do you love him?' 'I think so.' 'Good.'

I drove off, happy that I'd carry

The good news to Denise—released!

She took it quietly, but seemed pleased.

3

Her quietness said, could she believe me?

While driving home I still felt good,

But seeing Maureen cried, 'Don't leave me!'

And wept, it was like the Wye in flood.

I felt it was too great a leap from

Having a woman to escape from.

I knew with Maureen I was safe,

Divorced, but still my caring wife.

But she, to my distress, was craving

Some happiness! And so with 'Don,

Your toast!' as usual waiting on

The stairs for me, she was soon leaving.

I sobbed again, signing a cheque;

We hugged, and then she left with Jack.

4

I knew that she was right to do so.

Denise and Ross would come before

Too long, with, so to speak, her trousseau,

Three cats, a dog, a budgerigar.

I fought to conquer my depression

By thinking there would be a fusion

Of wife and mistress. Others could

Find having the one woman good;

And she was really a whole coven,

Hourly to touch up, sure it led

To what supremely comforted...

And she'd be happy... We could move, in

A few months to Cornwall, where my heart

Yearned to return to. A new start.

5

But still, I paced my own museum,

Or stood by children's beds, alone.

No, it was now a mausoleum

With things they'd loved and I'd not known,

Too workaholic, too *in absentia*,

Into my children's minds to venture.

No, still worse, a necropolis.

I was responsible for this.

My sole companion, little Thomas

Miaowed across my typewriter;

If I had left it up to her

My novel *Summit* might be famous;

In sorrow I bashed out my farce

Zombie-like, couldn't give an arse.

6

'Oh, you look awful! Let me, dear fellow,

Help you take off your overcoat,'

Said 'Speedy' Davies, slow and sallow.

'No time to lose! I'll operate

On Sunday morning.' I'd gone private,

Doubtful that I would be alive at

The point, far off, the NHS

Could optimistically guess

He'd see me, though the tests were showing

Stones in both kidneys. 'The right one,

Which looks less damaged by the stone.'

'The left?' He mumbled: 'There's no knowing...

Next year...' He didn't say it but

Clearly he gave it up... *kaput.*

7

But then a blessing, unexpected,

Thanks to a good deed I had done

To a Jewish author, well-connected,

Before my illness had begun:

I'd let her come and interview me,

And then immediately screw me.

I'd no desire, being depressed,

It was good manners to a guest;

I sensed she would feel disappointment

Leaving unfucked; why not be kind?

She liked it and, alarmed to find

My life at risk, fixed an appointment

In Harley Street: no cut, both saved,

No lengthy weakness to be braved.

8

I'd dared to mention lithotripsy

To 'Speedy'. 'Six months waiting list,'

He'd gloomed. Not true: close to collapse, I

Travelled to London. Treated fast,

I woke from the first operation

Feeling huge hunger and elation.

Denise soon rang, to share delight.

'I rang them every hour last night!

Took him three hours, he said, to hoick it

Out through the keyhole!' 'Are you dressed

For school?' 'Why, yes.' She chuckled, guessed.

'Move the phone down there close and pluck it!'

A moment, then I heard the *twang*,

So clear! My mind and body sang.

9

The staghorn op... It's hell when the soma's

Asleep still, yet the mind's alert.

The sister said, 'Oh, Mr Thomas!'

Rolling me with her, buxom, pert.

No life still as she scolded, squatting,

'Don't look up my skirt!' Then batting

Her eyes at me, as if to flirt,

'That nurse was looking up my skirt!'

I struggled with my tongue and mumbled,

'Luck-y.' Corpselike, I could see

The gap from blackhosed knee to knee.

On what would stir life she had stumbled.

The surgeons caused the stone to shift

But that girl had the Lazarus gift.

10

We came to live near where my parents

And ancestors lived so long ago.

They'd have approved Denise's clearance

Of wild ground to make flowers grow.

It might have been a different planet

I'd come home to—I'd thought; one cannot

Step into the same river twice.

Our contacts were genteel and... *nice*,

Incomers, no Cornish wit and passion.

With Ross unhappy at his school

I thought to make a swimming pool

To help him find friends. My depression

Affected him and (still) my wife.

It took an age to make a life.

11

I liked to think our house, in Moresk,

Is where once Tristan and Yseult lay

When they found haven in the forest.

They might have tried a different way.

Literature would have lost a magic

Tale, but it might have been less tragic

For the two Yseults, Tristan, Mark,

If they had chosen, not the dark

Path to the *Liebestod*, but a cluster,

All four entangling at Castle Dor.

They might have reached a safer shore

Than that evoked by the Bayreuth master.

Fidelity, but with added spice.

It's something we tried briefly, twice.

12

The first occasion...It felt mystic,

Not carnal. I found I liked to share

Denise. Was it simply masochistic

To feel a warmth observing her

Enjoying worship? Promiscuous fingers

In her, her dreamy response still lingers:

'I'm feeling pampered.' I first inside,

And then to watch... another's... glide

Into her, slowly disappearing,

Was the fearful ecstasy a mountaineer

Must feel as he hangs upon the sheer

Eiger North Face. By seeing, hearing,

I felt her pleasure being filled,

And his, silkily sucked in and held.

13

Foursomes are insecure and flaky,

As some will always want it more

And others less; but in my psyche

It was a thrill, a distant shore,

That always had made my heart beat faster.

Thought flies to Oedipus and Jocasta.

In 'Beverly' there were four of us;

Dad might be powerful but I was

Her beloved son. Hence zelophilia,

Excitement found in jealousy,

And there were ghosts that haunted me.

Add Lois—as it were Ophelia...

I don't think I shall ever go

Far from that tiny bungalow.

14

The second time, in Cornwall... Quickly

I came—my body—for really I

Was elsewhere. With a strange, half-sickly,

Weak feeling, suddenly childlike, shy,

Just yards from me the haunting vision,

My love in the flurry of coition,

Moved by a curious awe, I crawled

Across to where Denise was sprawled

Back on the sofa; he was kneeling,

Enwrapped by her large thighs. His wife

Lay back, I hope pleased well enough.

I stroked Denise to share their feeling

Of ecstasy. She: "Don, fuck off!"

And he: "You've had my wife—piss off!"

15

As King Mark might have done to Tristan

I literally pulled him out of her;

Forty and fit, he stuck a fist in

My stomach, depriving me of air.

I hit him back, bare-knuckle fighting,

I in my fifties! And delighting

Myself with one blow on his chin

Which made him reel. But I'd have been

Slain, had Denise not taken over,

With several punches to my left eye.

I slept till morning; Denise, spry:

'Great, to be fought for by two lovers!'

We laughed; she bathed my eye, and took

A photo of it—'For your next book!'

16

And partly through it we knew passion

Again, after some twenty years.

One night fucked, without intermission,

Until the dawn blanked out the stars.

We simply could not live sedately

Nor, in bed, make love moderately,

And needed to have an extra charge.

Time paused that night to watch us merge.

I was in love again quite madly.

She murmured to me, as dawn broke,

'I'll say this, you're a bloody good fuck!'

I'd have that as my epitaph gladly;

Not many couples, I would claim,

Have fallen in love for the third time.

17

Our old Welsh friends were amused, shaken,

Seeing us walk on windswept strands

When visiting us: could be mistaken,

They said, for teenagers, holding hands.

The transformation was amazing;

I can remember standing gazing

At her, on entering a bookshop;

She was immersed, did not look up;

I felt I'd never seen such beauty

And blessed by God that she was mine,

Her features thoughtful, classic, fine,

Her hair short, jet-black. Looking out I

Loved watching her, thickened, an old skirt

On, planting, feet planted in dirt.

18

And the years passed; in flint earth softened

By her hard labour our cairn Sam

Was in her much-loved blanket coffined

To comfort her; replaced by Tam,

Another cairn who gnawed my papers,

And we enjoyed her runs and capers

On beaches. Lust softened too; I wrote,

Novels, and then full of doubt

A biography of Alexander

Solzhenitsyn, whom I revered,

But joyous creation disappeared

As research I was buried under.

Denise took care of bread and salt

And Ross, his teen years difficult.

19

But then came happenings too cruel,

Made worse by my being a great fool:

Caitlin's firstborn, her precious jewel,

Alex, fell in our swimming pool—

Since then a sunken memorial garden.

Later, my mind began to harden

When after plenty a drought came;

She, sleeping in a separate room,

Blamed neck pain, tiredness. Yet for hours

I'd see her in the garden use

Her strength, so that seemed an excuse,

Our bed less crucial than her flowers.

I plunged, through anger and despair,

Into a passionate affair.

20

Beyond all measure and all prudence,

As if possessed by Circe's spells,

On a Greek isle with writing students

Where, en route to the Dardanelles,

Rupert Brooke perished of a fever,

A woman comely, lively, clever,

Charmed me, and could help me with my book

On Solzhenitsyn, as she spoke

Street-Russian. Soon I would go, tearful,

For I'd confessed and Denise raged,

To where my hurt would be assuaged,

Then soon steal home to what was fearful,

Her wrath, but real. I'd plead with her:

'This won't last, be patient for a year.'

21

And then—the memory is searing—

I'm reading, eating my sandwich lunch,

Ross, frantic, suddenly appearing,

Shouting, as I more slowly munch,

'Mum's in hospital! That bloody doctor!

Her neck is braced, it's a stress fracture!'

Then, when I visit her that night

Her jet-black hair has turned to white

And she's on tubes to help her breathing.

My God! The most enormous fear,

All other women disappear.

Ah, the wrong room... emotions seething,

I reach her as she's being assured

They don't think cancer. My God, that word...

22

'Physio. And not smoking would relieve it.'

At physio they'd touched, withdrew,

Sent her for x-ray. They couldn't believe it,

Half of her spine was eaten through.

She had to have a helmet fitted,

Screwed in her skull. And she had greeted

The surgeon, amazed she could move and stand,

With 'I guess it'll be harder to find

Men as turned on by this as stockings

And suspenders!' Ah, her wit's defence,

Like 'What a job, staring up women's cunts!'

Being stitched after birthing Ross; and shocking

To silence a pupil, his mouth a foul ditch,

By agreeing, 'I *am* a fucking bitch!'

23

I hoped and prayed my amorous madness

Would end. It did. That saved my soul.

Easier to live with untempered sadness.

I called from a Heathrow hotel

After a trip abroad; she sounded

Pleased—gentle—and I felt unbounded

Love for her, tenderness restored.

Amid grief I felt grace, a word

That's out of fashion, just as sin is;

I'd deeply sinned, but by God's grace

Broke through to vision out of haze,

Like having our first view of Venice

Crossing from Yugoslavia

In youth, amazed by it, in awe.

24

Grieving but sane, I could thenceforward

Give to her all my heart, all love.

Still saw the other, being a coward,

From time to time, so conscious of

The loneliness that would come later,

The house of silence, all the greater

As Ross had, through the internet,

Found love with a mother surrogate

In Canada. The awful sadness

Of that departure. I took them to

The station, howling my way through

The streets back, and to add to madness

My car horn stuck, and it too howled

Through the short journey, uncontrolled.

25

If we had made love passionately

She sadly pointed out to me,

Her body shaken almost nightly,

I would have had no cause to stray

But she'd have soon been quadriplegic.

Fate had decreed for us that tragic

Paradox. To conceive of her

Paralysed too was too much to bear.

In pain at night, she left me sleeping,

Save once, stretching her hand to cleave

To mine, and asking did I believe

In life after death. I'd trouble keeping

Steady my voice, said I thought time

Unreal, so yes. She seemed to calm.

26

We talked—I of her absence frightened—

She in a hospice. I'd sell our house

I said. She, thoughtfully: 'You mightn't

Like somewhere that's not full of us,

No memories.' It was agonising.

Then something comforting and surprising,

Since she was always reticent,

'Were I to live again I'd want

To live it differently, but still I

Would want to live my life with you.'

I grieved for her self-loss, yet knew

I myself would not live on fully;

How could I bear that there would be

An amputation of half of me?

27

I don't know how we mortals bear it,

Being with a loved one who will die,

Mid-life, for in a sense you share it,

But each is grieving differently.

It's something that I found unbearable

Yet knowing it was far more terrible

(Though that was hard to comprehend)

For her, for whom the world would end

Wholly. Our deep thoughts came out rarely;

She said she'd sometimes wished me dead

So guilt tormented her. I said,

'You knew I had the same wish, surely,

For you at times? No need for guilt,

It's not the way we truly felt.'

28

They said her strong imagination

Was why she was feeling so much fear

Of death—enjoy the relaxation

Of foot massages; life is here

And now. And also think of sharing

Your history with Anne, our caring

Helper, an author published locally

Who'll give it to your family.

Well yes, I wouldn't disagree with

The charge that she had far too strong

An imagination. It was wrong

To grieve she would no longer be with—

In her words—'mum, and you, and Ross'.

She shouldn't have tried to look across.

29

I can still hear her shout, 'This fucking

Place, not allowed a fucking fag!'

At eight wheeled from the hospice smoking

Room to be put to bed; a drag

To wheel her back again, for dying

Patients should be sedately lying.

She had never looked more beautiful,

Our love entirely spiritual;

The fetishistic items buried,

While what they symbolised shone through

As they were always meant to do

And we were glad to be still married

By mischance and to have a son

To bear our *hieros gamos* on.

30

I visited a stout clairvoyant;

It started badly when she said

I didn't look exactly buoyant,

And why was that? 'She's fucking dead!

My wife!' Good God, no Nostradamus!

Then she struck gold—our dead dog Sam was

With her, also a child who'd passed,

And had me weeping at the last,

Her gaze as if intently on her:

'She says you caused each other pain,

Both foolish; had she her life again

She'd live it in a different manner

But want to spend it still with you.'

'She *told* me that!' 'And it's still true.'

Front cover design by Chris Bond, utilising an illustration by Pete Hawley for a magazine advertisement for Jantzen, 1953.

Photographs on the back cover show:
Top left - a wedding party with, left to right, the author, a matron of honour, an uncle, Ray, Lois, the author's father and his mother.
Top right - the author kitted out to defend the realm.

Further Titles

Hunters in the Snow
By D.M. Thomas

Vienna in the early 20th century was, in the words of our protagonist and narrator, a soulless, syphilitic whore of a city; a turbulent and bubbling melting pot of races, creeds and politics, rapidly expanding as it strained to contain the ever-increasing multitudes. In such places the nightmare moments of modern history are conceived. This novel is a fictionalised account of those who were to change the very collective psyche of mankind. It is a vivid and poignant portrayal of the sometimes thin dividing line between becoming good or evil.

D. M. Thomas is a British novelist and poet, born and living in Cornwall. His novel *The White Hotel* was an international bestseller and shortlisted for the Booker Prize. It is rightly considered a modern classic, translated into more than 30 languages. John Updike said of the book: 'Astonishing ... A forthright sensuality mixed with a fine historical feeling for the nightmare moments in modern history, a dreamlike fluidity and quickness'; the statement could equally be applied to *Hunters in the Snow*.

Paperback, 164 pages. ISBN 978 1 908878 19 9. Also available on Kindle.

All Cornwall Thunders at My Door: A Biography of Charles Causley
By Laurence Green

All Cornwall Thunders at My Door is the first full biography of Charles Causley to be published, originally published to coincide with the 10th anniversary of his death in 2003. Laurence Green has compiled a great deal of information concerning Causley's life in Cornwall and beyond, of his personal history, his influences and motivations, helping to give context to the great legacy left to us by "the greatest poet laureate we never had."

"This is the first biography of Charles Causley, and takes us towards the heart of a marvellous poet and deeply intriguing man. It's all well done: clear, sympathetic, appreciative and shrewd. Everyone who loves Causley's poems will want to read it." — *Sir Andrew Motion*

"...it has been meticulously researched using archive material and the personal reminiscences of people in Launceston and elsewhere who knew Causley. Covering his early life, wartime service, teaching career and the years of success, Green provides not only a truthful overview of this literary giant but does so in the most entertaining of styles." — *Simon Parker, The Western Morning News*

Includes photographs not previously published and a foreword by Dr Alan M. Kent. Paperback, 220 pages. ISBN 978 1 908878 08 3. Also available on Kindle.

The Last Waltz: Poems
By D.M. Thomas

In both his poetry and his novels, such as the iconic world-bestseller *The White Hotel*, D.M. Thomas has followed his own vision, ignoring the fashionable and the expected. The Last Waltz is no exception. The impression it leaves is of experience, personal and historical, distilled over a life stretching from the threat of Hitler to the threat to freedom of thought and speech today. The moods vary, from grief to controlled anger to satirical humour; the themes, from falling in love on his first day at Infants school to a royal wedding competing in our news (successfully) with Palestinians being massacred. All explored with immense assurance in a rich variety of forms.

"There aren't many poets in England as good as Thomas." — *The Guardian*.

D.M. Thomas is an internationally known poet and novelist. His third novel, *The White Hotel*, considered a modern classic, has been translated into more than thirty languages. He lives in his native Cornwall with his fourth wife Angela.

Paperback, 94 pages. ISBN 978 1 908878 22 9.

A Complete History of Cornwall
By Thomas Cox

Transcribed from an original copy, published in 1720 by Thomas Cox as part of *Magna Britannia et Hibernia, Antiqua & Nova*, this new edition of Cox's rare partwork *A Compleat History of Cornwal* is a faithful reproduction of the original and contains a topographical description of Cornwall, as well as accounts of the Earls and Dukes of Cornwall and other worthies, the Natural History, an Ecclesiastical History and learned divines, an account of the parliamentary boroughs and corporations and a comprehensive gazetteer. This new edition, produced to commemorate the 300th anniversary of the original, also features all of the original illustrations, including Robert Morden's contemporary map of Cornwall, and has an Introduction by Chris Bond.

Paperback, 156 pages. ISBN 978 1 908878 15 6.

Corona Man: A Fictional Verse Journal in the Plague Year
By D.M. Thomas

John Trenear, an 84 year old widower, lives alone in a bleak London tower block. He has turned away from a world he finds alien, its customs and beliefs so different from the Christian simplicities of his Cornish childhood. He tweets not, neither does he watch TV. Consequently, when the coronavirus strikes and lockdown is imposed, he has no idea what is happening; Corona to him means only the fizzy soft drink he enjoyed as a child. On VE Day there are no Corona bottles being opened with an explosion of fizz, as they had in the merry street party he remembers: indeed the streets below his flat are incomprehensibly empty. But the day brings him added confusion and distress, for it appears that something called a 'hate crime' has been committed. *Corona Man*, a study of old age, confusion and isolation, is both very poignant and very funny.

D. M. Thomas is an internationally known poet and novelist. His third novel, *The White Hotel*, considered a modern classic, has been translated into more than thirty languages. He lives in his native Cornwall with his fourth wife Angela. Being incompetent at gardening, trying out new recipes or assembling giant jigsaw puzzles, he has spent the months of lockdown writing this fictional verse journal.

Paperback, 124 pages. ISBN 978 1 908878 18 2. Also available on Kindle.

Following 'An Gof': Leonard Truran, Cornish Activist and Publisher
By Derek R. Williams

Len Truran was, until his death in 1997, a highly influential figure within the fields of politics and culture in Cornwall. He joined Mebyon Kernow in 1964 and, over the years, acted as both secretary and chairman of the party. His publications, under the imprint of Dyllansow Truran, are widely recognised as being seminal in the story of Cornish publishing.

In this book Derek R. Williams explores the life of Len Truran, from his childhood through to his pivotal role in Mebyon Kernow and the campaign for the creation of a Cornish Assembly and on to the remarkably prolific and influential publisher he became.

"Derek Williams is to be congratulated for his handling of a most diverse and complex subject ... Leonard Truran was a dynamic force, active from the 1960s onwards in raising the sense of pride in Kernow through diverse means ... Derek Williams's well organised, highly readable book will preserve his memory for generations to come." — *Donald Rawe, The Cornish Banner.*

Paperback, 104 pages. ISBN 978 1 908878 14 4.

Gathering the Fragments: The Selected Essays of a Groundbreaking Historian
By Charles Thomas

This selection of work by the late Professor Charles Thomas, Cornwall's leading historian at the time of publication, focuses on the more elusive titles from his long and illustrious career and covers the whole range of his output from folklore and archaeology to military and local history, and from cerealogy to cryptozoology. The book also includes unpublished material, as well as specially composed introductions to each chapter, a full biography and a select bibliography.

Chapters featured include: A Plea for Neutrality (*New Cornwall*, 1955); Youthful Ventures Into the Realm of Folk Studies - Present-day Charmers in Cornwall (*Folk-Lore*, 1953), Underground Tunnels at Island Mahee, County Down (*Ulster Folklife*, 1957), Archaeology and Folk-life Studies (*Gwerin*, 1960); What Did They Do When it Rained in 1857? (*The Scillonian*, 1986); Home Thoughts from Abroad (*Camborne Wesley Journal*, 1948); The Day That Never Came (*The Cornish Review*, 1968); *Camborne Festival Magazine* - The Camborne Printing and Stationery Company (1971), The Camborne Students' Association (1974), Camborne's War Record, 1914-1919 (1976), The Camborne Volunteer Training Corps in World War One (1983), Carwynnen Quoit (1985); Jottings from Gwithian (*The Godrevy Light*) - How Far Back Can We Go? (2006), Ladies of Gwithian (2007); Two Funeral Orations (unpublished) - Charles Woolf (1984), Rudolf Glossop (1993); Archaeology and the Mind (unpublished) (1968 inaugural lecture, University of Leicester); The Archaeologist in Fiction (1976); Archaeology, and the Concept of Cornishness (unpublished) (1995 memorial lecture, Cornwall Archaeological Society); A Couple of Reviews - Lost Innocence: Archaeologists as People (*Encounter*, 1981), The Cairo Trilogy (*Literary Review*, 2001); An Impromptu Ode - To A.L. Rowse (1997); *The Cerealogist* - An Archaeologist's View (1991), Magnetic Anomalies (1991/92); Two Cryptozoological Papers - The "Monster" Episode in Adomnan's Life of St. Columba (*Cryptozoology*, 1988), A Black Cat Among the Pictish Beasts? (*Pictish Arts Society Journal*, 1994).

Professor Charles Thomas CBE DL DLitt FBA FSA was a former President of the Council for British Archaeology, the Society for Medieval Archaeology, the Royal Institution of Cornwall, the Cornwall Archaeological Society, the Cornish Methodist Historical Society and The John Harris Society.

"Most of us know of Charles Thomas through his major contributions to our knowledge of the early medieval period. But none of this work, save for two important contributions on cryptozoology, appears in this book. Instead we are treated to a range of material, both published and unpublished, on other matters that have attracted his interest. Cornwall, unsurprisingly, is a major theme but without anything from the journal *Cornish Archaeology*. Here the pieces are from publications such as *The Scillonian, Camborne Festival Magazine* and *The Godrevy Light*. And the range is as eclectic as the sources. Local and military history, folklife, biography, a review of fiction, crop circles, even his previously unpublished inaugural lecture as professor of archaeology at Leicester, all make an appearance. The book concludes with biographical details and a select bibliography. There is much here that you will not have read before, and it's full of wonderful and unexpected revelations." —
David Clarke, British Archaeology 127.

"Subtitled The Selected Essays Of A Groundbreaking Historian, it not only pays tribute to the breadth of Cornwall's leading historian's scholarship but is also an anthology in which every one of its two dozen or more pieces burns with the author's love for his native land and emphasises the fact that if anyone deserves to be now wearing the mantle of the late A L Rowse as our "greatest living Cornishman", then it has to be Professor Charles Thomas. As engaging as it is erudite and as rich, this is a book which should be on the menu of any reader with an interest in Cornwall and all things Cornish." — *Frank Ruhrmund, Western Morning News.*

Edited by Chris Bond. Paperback, 216 pages. ISBN 978 1 908878 03 8.

Cornwall's Historical Wars
By Rod Lyon

Rod Lyon, BBC Radio Cornwall presenter and former Grand Bard of the Gorsedh Kernow, takes the reader on a fascinating journey through the ages, and through the forgotten wars between the Cornish and their old enemies, the English, revealing a history not taught in schools, and one missing from the 'official' history books. From the early wars with the Saxons, through the rebellions of 1497 and 1549, and on to the Civil War, Rod traces the bloody events which helped to shape the culture and national identity of the Cornish people. This book is essential reading for all those who want to learn the truth about Cornwall's hidden history.

Paperback, 112 pages. ISBN 978 1 908878 05 2.

Cornwall
By Thomas Moule

Thomas Moule's topographical account of Cornwall is taken from the 1838 edition of The English Counties Delineated and is full of detail concerning the seats of the gentry, the monuments in the churches, the history of the parishes and boroughs and the numbers of houses and inhabitants. This fully-indexed edition is a useful source of information for local historians and for those interested in the Cornwall of 170 years ago. The cover of the book features part of Thomas Moule's map of Cornwall taken from the original edition.

Paperback, 186 pages. ISBN 978 0 9522064 6 0. Also available on Kindle.

The Fifties Mystique
By Jessica Mann

Many young women 'long to put the clock back to the post-war years when life seemed prettier and nicer.' In this book Jessica Mann demolishes such preconceptions about their mothers' or grandmothers' young days, showing that in reality life was uglier and nastier.

Born just before WW2, she grew up in the post-war era of austerity, restrictions and hypocrisy, before anyone even dreamed of Women's Lib. The Fifties Mystique is both a personal memoir and a polemic. In explaining the lives of pre-feminists to the post-feminists of today, Mann discusses the period's very different attitudes to sex, childbirth, motherhood and work, describes how she and other young women lived in that distant world with its forgotten restrictions and warns against taking hard-won rights for granted.

Jessica Mann was the author of 22 crime novels and 4 non-fiction books. As a journalist she had written for national newspapers, weeklies and glossy magazines and was the crime fiction critic of *The Literary Review*.

"Jessica Mann analyses the decade with forensic precision – stripping away the rose-coloured specs for good" — *The Daily Mail*

"thoughtful and emphatic ... a richly readable and persuasive piece of work" — *Penelope Lively, The Spectator*

an "excellently readable book" — *Katharine Whitehorn*

"Her battle cry is full of vivid descriptions of the grim, snobbery and casual misogyny of postwar Britain. A crime-writer by trade, her barely veiled exasperation only makes the polemic more enjoyable ... " — *The Mail on Sunday*

"an extremely engaging read: revealing, touching, informative and occasionally comic." — *Simon Parker, The Western Morning News*

"She recalls the grime of the 50s: endless stinking nappy buckets; smog; inadequate washing facilities; body odour whenever people were crowded together. She recalls boredom and isolation, and suspects both the child-rearing experts and the government of a concerted push to get mothers back home after the war, so that there would be jobs for the returning 'boys'. And she recalls the unacceptability of talking, or sometimes even knowing, about sex, female anatomy, and cancer. She is bang on" — *Baroness Neuberger, The Jewish Chronicle*

First published by Quartet Books in 2012.
Paperback, 224 pages. ISBN 978 1 908878 07 6.

The Wheal Margaret Adventure: A Calendar of Agents' Reports and Associated Records, 1857 to 1875
By Chris Bond

A calendar of Agents' Reports, Correspondence and Mine Reports relating to Wheal Margaret Mine in the parish of Lelant in West Cornwall. The records transcribed here date from 1857, shortly after the mine was re-opened, up to 1875, shortly after the decision was made to quit the adventure. They give a detailed account of the workings of each lode in the mine; the promise and the problems; the fortunes and the failings. Any comprehensive series of reports such as this provides a valuable historical background to the story of tin mining in Victorian Cornwall. Edited and with an introduction by Chris Bond, who previously edited the catalogue of the Boulton & Watt papers held at the Cornwall Record Office, and who additionally transcribed a substantial part of the same.

Paperback, 130 pages. ISBN 978 1 908878 15 1.

Dowsing
By Thomas Fiddick

This reprint of a rare and obscure pamphlet, originally published by Thomas Fiddick of Camborne in 1913, details the various experiments which he undertook whilst dowsing for mineral lodes in his native Cornwall, as well as giving a potted history of mineralogical dowsing in the area. It also gives details of his "Dowsing Cone" and instructions for its use. This book is an invaluable resource for those who study or practise the art of rhabdomancy, or for those who wish to learn more concerning the history of mining in Cornwall. Edited and with an introduction by Chris Bond.

"Great stuff! … fascinating." — *Professor Charles Thomas.*

Paperback, 44 pages. ISBN 978 0 9522064 8 4.

Dead Woman Walking
By Jessica Mann

Gillian Butler moved away from Edinburgh 50 years ago, or so her friends thought. When her murdered body is found, they must try to remember who last saw her alive. Perhaps it was Isabel, now a novelist and people-tracer, or the twice widowed Hannah, or the psychiatrist, Dr Fidelis Berlin, an expert on child abuse, abandonment, abduction and adoption, who had herself been an unidentified infant rescued from Nazi Germany and now hopes to discover her real name at last. Fidelis Berlin and other characters from Mann's earlier books reappear in this tense, gripping tale of vengeance, family ties and the mystery of identity.

Jessica Mann was the author of 22 crime novels and 4 non-fiction books. As a journalist she had written for national newspapers, weeklies and glossy magazines. She was the crime fiction critic of *The Literary Review*. Jessica and her late husband, the archaeologist Professor Charles Thomas, lived in Cornwall.

"This is a complex and chilling story, with many shifts of perspective and timeframe. The quality of the writing shines out. The question of changing identity is crucial — not just of individuals but of women in British society over the last half-century. Beneath it all is an elegiac note of regret, a sense of wrong choices with long consequences." — *Andrew Taylor, The Spectator*

"As ever with this author, the intelligent (and complex) texture of the novel matches its sheer storytelling nous." — *Barry Forshaw, crimetime.co.uk*

"Engaging, enthralling and hugely entertaining." — *Frank Ruhrmund, Western Morning News*

"There is a very striking climax, but this is also a novel of ideas, about feminism, family and literature … As you would expect with Jessica Mann, it's a very well-written as well as a poignant book, and I'm delighted to have read it." — *Martin Edwards, Do You Write Under Your Own Name?*

Paperback, 192 pages. ISBN 978 1 908878 06 9.

Godmanstone Blues
By Chris Bond and Andy Paciorek

Defy not the urge to buy! For this book could save your very living soul.

Poetry and prose by Chris Bond, with original illustrations by the acclaimed artist Andy Paciorek.

Paperback, 100 pages. ISBN 978 1 908878 17 5. Also available on Kindle.

Chinese Whispers
By Andrew Birtles

Dear Reader, you probably know the party game "Chinese Whispers" but if you don't here's what happens. A group of your friends and family get together, someone starts off with a sentence, in this case "Piglets in pyjamas danced on tiptoes round a tree". Then they whisper to the next person who whispers what they heard to the next and so on and so on...

You'll find it changes every time because people don't hear properly what's been said. Oh, and by the way, you'll be the last person to hear the message so listen very carefully while you're reading this book because without you there won't be a final page.

Yours sincerely, Andrew Birtles

P.S. You may be unfamiliar with some of the words used, so brief descriptions have been included to enhance your enjoyment.

Paperback, full colour, 52 pages. ISBN 978 1 908878 09 0. Also available on Kindle.

Shut away!: My early days fishing out of Newquay
By Rod Lyon

Rod Lyon, former Grand Bard of the Gorsedh Kernow, recollects his early days fishing out of Newquay, "in the days before modern electronic aids, man-made fibre ropes, twines and cords, plastic 'skins' and floats instead of cork ... when navigation to and from the gear was by dead reckoning, using only a watch and a compass, with only experience telling you what to allow for with the tide." Rod illustrates, in both words and pictures, the techniques and the equipment used in those bygone days, and along the way remembers some of the more notable characters, both Cornish and Breton, who frequented 'down Quay'. The book also includes a gazetteer of his favourite fishing grounds.

Paperback, 120 pages. ISBN 978 1 908878 01 4.

Antiquarian Notes on the Prehistory of Cornwall
Edited by Chris Bond

This is the first volume in a series dedicated to reproducing some of the long-forgotten articles from historical journals relating to Cornwall's illustrious and ancient past. The articles themselves are taken from a variety of publications, both local and national, and from a wide span of time. To have these valuable sources in a set of compact volumes makes not only for an interesting read but also a useful tool for reference. This initial volume includes: Account of Antiquities discovered in Cornwall, by the Rev. Malachy Hitchins (*Archæologia* 15, 1806); Pendarvis Quoit, Cornwall by J. S. Storer and J. Greig (*Antiquarian and Topographical Cabinet*, 1808); The Hurlers (*Light From the West*, 1833); Some Account of the Opening of a Barrow near Newquay by The Rev. Canon Rogers (*Report of the Royal Institution of Cornwall*, 1840); King Arthur's Hall by S. R. Pattison (*Report of the Royal Institution of Cornwall*, 1852); The Celtic and Other Antiquities of the Land's End District of Cornwall by Richard Edmonds (*Archæologia Cambrensis*, 1857-8); Notes on Stone Circles by J. T. Blight (*The Gentleman's Magazine*, 1868); Remarks on the Stone-Circles at Boscawen-un and Boskednan in West Cornwall by E. H. W. Dunkin (*The Reliquary Quarterly, Archælogical Journal and Review*, 1869-70); Cornish Antiquities Viewed in the Light of Modern Research by William C. Borlase (*Transactions of the Penzance Natural History and Antiquarian Society*, 1880-81); Duloe Stone Circle by C. W. Dymond (*Journal of the British Archaeological Association*, 1882); Prehistoric Remains in Cornwall: 1 - East Cornwall by A. L. Lewis (*Journal of the Anthropological Institute of Great Britain and Ireland*, 1896) and Note on an Unrecorded Cromlech in North Cornwall by Henry Dewey (*Journal of the Royal Institution of Cornwall*, 1911). The volume also contains a bibliography and an introduction by Chris Bond.

Paperback, 160 pages. ISBN 978 1 908878 21 2.

For further details see cornovia-press.wikidot.com

Printed in Great Britain
by Amazon